Bookmercial™ Marketing

Bookmercial™ Marketing

Why Books Replace Brochures In The Credibility Age

VICTOR CHENG

INNOVATION PRESS

SAN FRANCISCO

This book and the information contained herein are for informative purposes only. The information in this book is distributed on an "As Is" basis, without warranty. The author makes no legal claims, express or implied, and the material is not meant to substitute legal or financial counsel.

The author, publisher, and/or copyright holder assume no responsibility for the loss or damage caused, or allegedly caused, directly or indirectly by the use of information contained in this book. The author and publisher specifically disclaim any liability incurred from the use or application of the contents of this book.

All rights reserved. No part of this book may be reproduced or transmitted in any form by any means, electronic, mechanical, photocopying, recording, or otherwise, without the prior written permission of the publisher.

Throughout this book trademarked names are referenced. Rather than putting a trademark symbol in every occurrence of a trademarked name, we state that we are using the names in an editorial fashion only and to the benefit of the trademark owner with no intention of infringement of the trademark.

Copyright © 2008 Victor Cheng
All Rights Reserved

Published by Innovation Press, 182 Howard St, Suite #185, San Francisco, CA 94105

Printed in the United States of America

ISBN 10: 0-9764624-7-8
ISBN 13: 978-0-9764624-7-7

For Julia, Alex & Charlie

Preface

If all of your competitors lied in their marketing, would you lie in yours? If they exaggerated claims, over-promised, and under-delivered, would you? If you didn't, how would you compete against them?

My products had genuine advantages over my competitors, but my competitors claimed to offer the same thing. At worst they were lying. At best they were exaggerating.

When prospects are jaded (for good reasons), don't believe anything you have to say, and can't separate truth from fiction, what the heck are you supposed to do to compete and win?

These were the thoughts running through my head many years ago while I was leading a division of a publicly-traded technology company. At the time, the only strategy I could come up with was to be different in my marketing, offer more proof, and work like a dog hoping we'd win in the end.

While this "work harder" approach did work, I could not help but wonder at the time if there was a way to "work smarter." It took me seven years to realize that I completely misunderstood my problems—and to find a unique and different approach.

At the time, I thought I had a sales and marketing problem. In hindsight, I realized that was not the case at all. I had a better product. I had a better marketing message. I had excellent distribution. The problem was our prospects did not trust anything we had to say. We didn't have a marketing issue. We had a *lack of credibility* issue.

I realized that my company's ideal prospects had been burned, disappointed, and ripped off one too many times. To survive, they depended on developing a healthy sense of skepticism.

The bigger the promise we would make, the more they were skeptical. The harder we sold, the more they backed away. The louder we'd yell our marketing message to the marketplace, they more they resisted.

If doing more doesn't work and doing less certainly doesn't either, what does one do?

Answer: Do something different.

So I started doing some homework. What professions do people trust the most?

At the top of the list were: doctors, teachers, and professors. At the bottom of the list: used car salespeople, telemarketers, and with all the corporate scandals percolating in the media, CEOs.

Ouch. (Needless to say that's the day I stopped introducing myself as a CEO—heck I'd get more respect by introducing myself as a telemarketer.)

The message was clear: The more you sell (and act like you want their money), the less you're trusted.

So what did the professions at the top of the list—doctors, teachers, and professors—have in common?

Authority, knowledge, and expertise.

So I began thinking about this as it applied to myself. I was certainly extremely knowledge about my clients, products, and services. I certainly had exceptional expertise—so why didn't prospects trust me, and my company, more?

In a word: authority.

Without authority, one's knowledge and expertise are dismissed. For example, medical doctors get their authority and power from their medical school diploma, medical license, and white lab coat. If you took someone who has more up-to-date knowledge and expertise than a doctor in certain diseases (which is quite possible with all the latest medical researched published online these days), but lacked all the trappings of authority, you have someone with knowledge and expertise that's largely getting ignored.

The final question I asked others and myself was, "In business, how do you know if someone is an authority-figure and an obvious expert in their field?" The consistent answer I got back was: they've published a book.

This was the big breakthrough. Publishing a book would put me in the same category as doctors, teachers and professors. Instead of being perceived as the chief salesperson of my company, I would be perceived as the chief teacher a much more trusted role. My sales staff would shift from being perceived as annoying sales pests to welcomed "teaching assistants."

The rest of this book reveals how and why book publishing is a radical "game changer" in the world of marketing. It was the "work smarter" method I was looking for seven years ago, but did not discover until more recently.

Through this journey I invented a special book format—the Bookmercial book—that's designed deliberately to weave extensive (but subtle) pre-selling strategies into the context of a *genuinely* useful book.

In the pages that follow, you'll discover the specific marketing and revenue growth challenges that book publishing solves. It's an approach to marketing and pre-selling complex products and services that you and your competitors are almost certainly ignoring. It's an approach that consciously and thoughtfully looks to earn a prospect's trust from the start—making the rest of your sales and marketing efforts easier and more effective immediately.

About The Author

Victor Cheng is the inventor of the Bookmercial book and an expert in using books to market and pre-sell complex products and services. He has two degrees from Stanford University and is a former McKinsey & Company consultant.

Victor has been a featured speaker at Harvard Business School and the MIT Sloan School of Business. He has also held CEO, CIO, and marketing executive positions in five public and privately-held companies.

CONTENTS

SECTION I: TRADITIONAL MARKETING IS BROKEN 1
   1) THE WORLD OF MARKETING HAS CHANGED PERMANENTLY 2
   2) TRADITIONAL MARKETING DOESN'T WORK IN THE NEW WORLD 20

SECTION II: AUTHORITY IN MARKETING 26
   3) THE FIVE SECRETS TO MARKETING IN THE NEW WORLD 28
   4) AUTHORITY-BASED MARKETING 34
   5) THE SEVEN WAYS TO BECOME AN AUTHORITY FIGURE 42
   6) THE #1 AUTHORITY-BUILDING TOOL 50

SECTION III: THE BOOKMERCIAL AS A MARKETING TOOL 60
   7) THE BOOKMERCIAL 62
   8) HOW TO GENERATE PUBLICITY 78
   9) HOW TO OBTAIN PUBLIC SPEAKING OPPORTUNITIES 84
   10) HOW TO GENERATE LEADS 88
   11) HOW TO CLOSE MORE SALES MORE QUICKLY .. 106

SECTION IV: HOW TO PRODUCE A BOOKMERCIAL 116

    12) A Bookmercial Isn't Written, It's Engineered 118
    13) How to Choreograph Bookmercial Content 132
    14) Writing a Bookmercial 138
    15) Printing and Distributing Your Bookmercial 152
    16) How to Get Started 158

SECTION V: RESOURCES 160

    17) Author Contact Information 162

Section I: Traditional Marketing Is Broken

CHAPTER 1

The World of Marketing Has Changed Permanently

The world around us continues to change at a faster and faster rate. The world of marketing has not been immune to this speed of change. If you continue to do the marketing that worked for you 10 years ago, you will find these efforts undermined for no visible reason. Behind this shift are five disturbing trends that will forever impact the options for how companies can market themselves.

You can choose to ignore these trends and have your business suffer without knowing why, or you can learn about and embrace these trends, and exploit them for your company's own benefit – leaving your competitors wondering why their marketing seems less and less effective each year.

Here are these five mega trends.

Mega Trend 1:
Advertising Overload

Advertising overload is a curse of our times. The volume of marketing, advertising, and sales messages coming at us from all directions overwhelms us. We can't escape it. What is happening instead is that we're tuning it all out. Rather than filtering the messages and determining what is and what isn't important, we are simply ignoring it all.

Telemarketers are a fine example. No one likes telemarketers interrupting him or her at dinnertime or any time really. It has finally become so intrusive that lawmakers have passed laws regulating cold calling. The "Do Not Call" list was part of this need to control the quantity of communications coming our way. There's also a "Do Not Fax" list, so you're not even allowed to fax information to prospective customers until they specifically ask for it. If you do, you can be fined or even prosecuted.

TIVO and digital video recorders have reduced the number of commercials we have to watch. That's great as a consumer, but as a business, it makes it tougher to get your message out, because no one has to sit through your commercials anymore.

E-mail is increasingly being regulated. While the number of e-mails promising you rock bottom prices on Viagra have been curtailed, many of these laws – combined with spam filters – have also restricted a business from sending legitimate e-mails to new prospects. Marketing-specific terms trigger spam filters, and these e-mails are automatically deleted or dumped into the junk folder without ever being seen.

For businesses trying to acquire new customers, this is putting a stranglehold on traditional marketing efforts.

The enemy is no longer your competitor – it is advertising overload and the things your prospects are putting in place to stop the clutter.

Sure, you could fall back on the old standby—direct mail. However, when the mailbox overflows with your mailing and 45 others, you'll be in the same boat. Your customers will become distracted by all the other mailings and not pay attention to your message.

It's a no-win situation. If you cut back on advertising, prospects will not be able to find you and revenue will drop, right? If you spend money on traditional advertising and people are tuning you out with TIVOs and spam filters, the same thing will happen anyway. The only difference is you'll end up spending money you don't have on marketing that no one is paying attention to in the first place.

Mega Trend 2: You Can't Trust Anyone Anymore

The age of distrust has seriously affected the way businesses can market their products and services. Even if claims are entirely true, people are loath to believe it. They've just been burned too many times by scandals, recalls, and government investigations. Even if you have a major breakthrough or a genuinely superior product, your prospects are trained to ignore it or simply not believe it.

Much of this age of distrust can be pinned on leaders of once unshakeable institutions. It wasn't so long ago that President Nixon claimed to a nation that he was not a crook. Two decades later, President Clinton lied about his relations with Monica Lewinsky. Other senators and representatives have been caught up in their own improprieties, from sex scandals and bribes to embezzlement and fraud.

Even our most sacred institutions have shattered our trust. Entire parishes went bankrupt as the Catholic Church settled mega-million dollar lawsuits in recent years. They aren't alone in the world of religion, either. For a while, a parade of evangelical ministers made endless confessions to their congregations, broadcast worldwide by satellite. Who can forget Reverend Jim Bakker's improprieties with Jessica Hahn, leading his successor, Jerry Falwell, to call him a "liar, an embezzler, and the greatest scab and cancer on the face of Christianity in 2,000 years of church history?"

Of course, there are the corporate scandals, such as those of Tyco, WorldCom, and, the poster child of all scandals, Enron. Not only was the public betrayed in all these highly publicized cases of wrongdoing, but also many investors lost their life savings as once sky-high stock prices dropped through the bottom.

Even the government's relatively loose truth in advertising laws recognizes this trend. The federal government enacted Puffery Laws that allow businesses to embellish and exaggerate in their advertising without it being illegal.

These laws, and I'm not a lawyer here, so you will want to check on this with your own counsel, allow you to legally exaggerate (which is really just a polite way of saying you're allowed to lie). The government, which nobody trusts in the first place, allows businesses to say, "we're number one," "we have the best selection," and "we're the best in town." Their rationale is that it's common knowledge that all companies exaggerate and boast. Since everyone knows this to be true and nobody believes what these companies say anyway, nobody gets hurt if they're permitted to exaggerate. So "puffery" or exaggeration is legal.

When you think about it, that's an amazingly sad state of affairs. The government we don't trust has told corporations that we have trouble trusting that they can lie (a little) in their advertising claims without fear of recourse, because we're all supposed to just know they're lying.

In short, the cards are already stacked against you when you are trying to market your products, services, or company. Your prospects are already wary of your claims because they have been let down by others who claimed to be telling the truth. Even if you are telling the absolute truth, no one will automatically believe it. Worse, they may not even be listening in the first place.

This is an important point to make. Even if you really have created the most amazing product or service in history, something that will change the world, the world is unlikely to take your claim at face value. Other advertisers have already beaten you to the punch and not delivered, and like the boy who cried "wolf" too many times, no one is likely to believe you just because you say it's so.

Mega Trend 3:
The Empowered and Informed Customer

If you're going to sell your product or service through traditional selling techniques, you're going to run afoul of savvy consumers who have already done research on their own. However, if you can become part of the education process and teach them how to shop and buy, you have the chance to improve your position in the marketplace. You'll become a trusted source of information, a teacher if you will.

Every day, Google.com processes nearly 100 million web searches. All of these searches are for information, with a significant portion being quests for information about businesses, products, and services. People are doing their homework these days, and these informed customers are changing the way we do business.

Perhaps at no time in our history has there been so much information at one's fingertips. Friends and family that saw something on the Internet about a product, service, or company are influencing people who don't even use the Internet.

First, customers have become really good at understanding products and services. In the old days, the salesperson did much of this work. The company was able to control the flow of information through sales pitches and brochure copy.

The Internet changed that. Today, the Internet is not only the salesperson, but it is also an encyclopedia of information, opinions, and critiques. These combine to create the knowledge base of your customer or your prospect. The bar has been raised in terms of expectations as a result.

This has certainly been true for me. Before I make any major purchase, I make sure I have conducted the proper research. I want to know what I'm getting and what others thought about the product or service I'm considering. I don't think I'm different from most executives these days. I want to know my options. I want to understand them. I want to make informed purchases.

The age of the informed customer is all too well known to healthcare professionals. Many doctors today are complaining that patients are bringing in reams of printouts from the Internet as they do research on every aspect of a disease, real or imagined. These self-diagnoses are driving doctors nuts. Instead of taking their advice (after long years in the practice, not to mention residency and schooling), patients are questioning everything the doctor says, quoting studies, clinical trials, and published papers. They want to know if their doctor is up on all the latest research, which may have been posted only two weeks ago. Right or wrong, this puts more power in the hands of the patient and puts the doctor on the defensive.

This mega trend of an increasingly informed customer is happening in every market. The Internet has only accelerated this mega trend to make it easy for customers to educate themselves. Online, there are thousands of product review and buyer guide websites. These sites have recognized this trend and are catering specifically to customers who want to be informed. This is very smart, because these sites help sway customers early in the buying process.

All of these resources – the online product reviews, the buying guides, and sites like Consumer Reports – have introduced a new dynamic into traditional sales and marketing processes. Sales and marketing used to be about a relationship between prospect and salesperson. Now, you have these educational "middlemen" or teachers appearing in the middle of a more traditional prospects-salesperson relationship.

What's intriguing is how often these educational "middlemen" that play the role of teacher (with the prospect taking on the role of student) have far more influence than the traditional salespeople. This is because most people trust teachers more than they trust salespeople. This fundamental trend is impacting how business is done and can't be ignored.

Mega Trend 4: The Messenger Is More Important Than the Message

In the past, knowledge was power. The person who knew how to do something (the butcher, baker, or candlestick maker) had economic power.

Then came books, radio, TV, and the Internet. Suddenly, anyone can access a wealth of information with a library card or the Internet. They can learn about virtually anything – how to cook, how to fix a car, ride a unicycle, perform surgery – anything.

The knowledge of how to be a butcher, baker, or candlestick maker is instantly available to anyone within a few keystrokes.

Today, the problem is that there is too much information. We don't have the time or energy to process and prioritize it all. We have compensated for this by seeking out others who can help us make sense of it all. They are our information filters. They tell us what is important and what's not. They help us manage the unmanageable.

It's funny how things have come full circle in some respects. While information is no longer controlled by the select few, we rely on a select few to tell us what information we should pay attention to, trust, and act upon. The messenger has become more important than the message.

Let me give you some examples.

E-mail: The "From" Line Is More Important Than the "Subject" Line

Here's a little example to prove my point. When you get an e-mail, do you look at the subject line or the sender's name first? Most of the time, people look at the sender's name first before deciding if they should look at the message. If the name isn't familiar, they may just delete the mail without even reading it.

I know this is the case with me. I get hundreds of e-mails every week. I don't have the time to look through them all. Instead, I look at the name of the person who sent it. If it's from a family member, friend, or colleague, I read it automatically regardless of the subject line or the content. It could just be a bunch of nonsense or random characters, but I'm still going to look at it because of the person who sent the e-mail. In contrast, the opposite is rarely true. I routinely ignore e-mails from people I don't know, even if they happen to discuss topics that I find interesting. Clearly, more so than ever, the messenger is much more important than the message.

Experts Are Taken More Seriously

This mega trend impacts every part of life, not just something as basic as e-mail.

For example, I went to the doctor recently for a checkup. He ran a battery of tests to evaluate my health. After doing all these tests, the doctor came back with the following recommendations: lose a few pounds and start exercising a bit more. You know what I did? I immediately changed my diet, exercised more, and dropped a few pounds within a month.

My wife had a good time with this, of course. She had been telling me exactly the same thing and asked why I didn't believe her. I thought about that for a while. It was because an authority figure had told me to do this – a doctor in a white lab coat – someone who looked like an expert. I believed that he knew what he was talking about and I acted upon it. He was a trusted expert.

Even though I love my wife, her counsel fell on deaf ears. It wasn't that I didn't respect her opinion; it's just that I trusted the doctor's expertise more. They both said virtually the same thing, but I ended up listening to someone who had all the trappings of being an expert on the subject of my health. I'm not proud of this, but I think you'll agree that it's a fairly common response.

I was on the receiving end of this once myself, so I can see how my wife felt. I was attending a lecture and when the guest speaker, an author and expert in his field, finished, he stayed afterwards to answer questions from the audience.

Following his talk, a bunch of us stayed after, huddling around him to ask more questions. I was somewhere in the middle of the group. A person in front of me asked a question that I happened to know the answer to, so I answered his question, even though he didn't direct his question to me. Rather than thank me, he turned around, gave me a nasty glare that said I was being rude for answering the question, and then turned his back on me. It was only after the speaker said that I was right that the person even acknowledged me ever so slightly. However, he still had that irritated look in his face.

I was only trying to be helpful, but this person looked at me like I was a nuisance. I had the correct information, but because I wasn't the perceived expert and didn't have any of the trappings of authority, my correct answer was ignored and rejected. He didn't even stop to consider its worth or accuracy. My answer was dismissed because he did not perceive me as an expert on the topic. Again, "who" says something is often more important than "what" is said.

Using the Authority of McKinsey & Company to Validate an Idea

Early on in my career, I was a management consultant at McKinsey & Company. McKinsey is fairly well known in Fortune 500 circles for a few reasons. First, the firm works with 75% of Fortune 500 and Global 500 CEOs. Second, more Fortune 500 CEOs are former McKinsey employees than former employees of any other employer in the world. In addition to me, former McKinsey consultants include the current and former CEOs of IBM, Campbell Soup, Sun Microsystems, Westinghouse, MTV Networks, Delta Airlines, American Express, and many other companies.

One of the things I found interesting about my client work is how often I would take a suggestion from a "low level" employee of my client that the CEO had previously ignored, put my and McKinsey's name on it, and get the idea adopted by the CEO. We would always be transparent that we got the idea from the CEO's staff, but until we "blessed" the idea, the CEO did not take it seriously.

At first, I thought this was an isolated situation of one CEO that wasn't paying attention, but I realized it was fairly consistent. I later discovered it was because for every one good idea the CEO hears from his staff (some 7 levels down in the corporate hierarchy), he would get 25 ideas that were useless or not practical. At the end of the day, it was information overload, so he or she would rely on McKinsey (an authority figure) to sift through all the ideas and present just the best ones.

Once again, we see the messenger matters more than the message.

The Only Thing More Influential Than an Expert Is a Celebrity Expert

The only thing better than being an expert is being a famous celebrity expert. Case in point: My wife and I have always been big on keeping track of how we spend our money. Even when we were students and didn't have much, we kept track of where every penny went.

Somewhere along the line, we lost the hard drive on the computer. All the data was gone and it was simply inconvenient to recreate everything we had in terms of budgets and tracking systems, so we put it off for a while. One day, my wife insisted it was time to get this all set up again and that we needed to keep track of all our spending.

What caused this sudden urge? It was a personal finance series on Oprah. An expert on personal finance was giving advice to the audience regarding how to manage money using the computer. Even though that person was a complete stranger, my wife decided she was an authority and should be listened to. After all, she was on Oprah and she had written a book about it.

It didn't matter that I was a big believer in this and had been doing the same thing until the computer crashed. Someone on Oprah said we needed to pay attention to this, now!

Personally, I thought it was funny that the personal finance expert on Oprah had a bigger impact on my wife than her finance professors at Harvard Business School. Once again, the identity and trust one has in a particular messenger is more influential than the message itself.

In an age of information overload, this reliance on the messenger is understandable. It is one of the ways we cope with the massive amount of data coming our way. Rather than ignore it entirely, we turn to others – authority figures, celebrities, and experts – to filter it for us. Rather than do the work ourselves, we let others that we respect and who appear to be "in the know" do it for us.

This has a tremendous impact on marketing. It means that your customers, clients, and prospects are having others do the filtering for them. Your messages have to get through another line of defense that you've never had to market to before. It's no longer enough to simply present the facts – differentiate yourself in the marketplace and advertise this to customers. Now, you have to get the messenger to provide the recommendation or become the trusted messenger yourself.

In the age of the messenger, the world has been turned on its head. The message is unimportant, unless a trusted messenger says it is. While we can get as much information as we need on virtually any topic, we don't have the tools, energy, or time to filter it all ourselves.

You may have something important to say, but until your prospects trust you first, it doesn't matter what you say. They either won't pay attention or they won't believe you.

Mega Trend 5:
Substance Matters More Than Ever

In an age of substance, it's no longer enough to say you're the best or the biggest. You have to back up everything you say. If you don't have the lowest price or the best service in town, your customers will find out. They'll do their research, listen to the people they trust, and filter out anything you say that runs counter to their intelligence-gathering process. The only way to avoid this is to have real substance. This means that you and your staff must deliver on your promises, back your products or services like you say you will, and ensure that you truly are different from your competitors. Fancy packaging and witty slogans won't sway people. Substance will.

The free flow of information makes comparison-shopping easy. This is particularly true in a world that is flat. To borrow a phrase from Thomas Friedman's book, "The world is flat; there are fewer borders around people; and products and services flow really effortlessly around the world because shipping, global e-commerce, money, products, and services flow around the globe very, very easily."

To stand out, you have to offer something different, but it's not good enough to just be different or even better. You have to be able to get the message across very clearly to your target audience about why you are different or better. In traditional marketing, it's almost impossible to do this in just 10 to 20 seconds. Twenty years ago, you could buy airtime on television and people would buy your product just because you had a nice jingle or slogan. Those days are over, of course. Not only is it hard to explain your project in neat little sound bites, but also you have to convince a jaded, informed person that he or she should use your product or service instead of the other guy's, even though it's nearly impossible to tell the difference between the two.

Want an example? Look at several car ads on TV. Can you tell the difference between the cars as they zoom down curving roads or spin around on wet pavement? They all look the same. In addition, the commercials don't even bother telling you the name of the car or even its maker until the very end. Even after you watch the commercial a dozen times, you still can't tell the difference between one silver car and another.

Of course, it doesn't really matter if you are different or better these days. It only matters what people know. If they never hear your story, then you're just like everyone else in the minds of your prospects. You can have a better mousetrap and be the only one to offer it, but if no one knows this, either because they are not listening or at least not listening to you, what's the point?

As you can see, the traditional ways of marketing are crumbling before our eyes. Prospects are overwhelmed with advertising, don't trust anyone, and insist on being educated before buying. Sadly, most traditional marketing only adds to the feeling of being overwhelmed with distrust and lack of useful education in the marketplace. In addition, when the identity of the messenger matters more than the words, and prospects demand that companies provide unique and substantial value to the market, most traditional marketing methods don't clearly and obviously address these two key needs. In short, traditional marketing is breaking down, and the impact is only going to get worse.

CHAPTER 2

Traditional Marketing Doesn't Work In The New World

The traditional marketing methods we've all relied on for more than a hundred years are beginning to fail us. Let's look at each of these methods and see how they stack up in this new world.

In the first chapters, we covered the five disturbing trends that are affecting traditional marketing. First, we talked about advertising overload in most markets. Second, we discussed how there is a tremendous amount of distrust out there among customers and prospects.

Third, we looked at how informed customers are these days, how they are doing more homework up front so that it's becoming harder to sway them by the time they're ready to buy. Fourth, we discussed the age of the messenger and how celebrity or authority can have more weight than the message. Finally, we talked about the age of substance, where you not only have to offer customers a better product, but you also have to get them to understand the differences and benefits in a time when they're either not listening at all or only listening to the people they trust.

Television Commercials – Let's Skip Them

Television and radio is a good place to start. The main problem with commercials on TV and radio is they all sound or look like commercials. The second the promotion starts, our filters kick in and we ignore it for the next 30 seconds or so. Entire industries, like digital video recorders, are dedicated to helping us ignore commercials. We are not only trained to ignore them, but we're developing ways to ignore them automatically.

The second problem with commercials is they are too short. In an age where cute jingles and slogans no longer sell, it's hard to earn the listener's trust or say what you have to say about your product to help them make an informed purchase. There's just not enough time.

Newspaper & Magazine Readers: Skip the Ads, Read the Articles

Newspapers and magazines are merely clutter. Thumb through a publication once and see for yourself. Your eyes simply pass by the ads; readership studies have confirmed this. When researchers tracked eye movements of subjects reading newspapers and magazines, they found that the subjects skipped right over the ads as they looked for articles instead.

Why do readers do this? Perhaps it is because it's instantly obvious that advertisers want the reader's money. This creates a level of immediate suspicion and distrust before the reader even opens the publication. True, there's more room in a display ad to tout your wares, but it's not enough to provide the level of education and product information necessary to spur a purchase.

Advertising is, of course, very expensive. Acquiring a new customer through ads in broadcast or print mediums is difficult to do well. The more you have to educate a customer, the more advertising you have to buy. At some point, the cost to get a new customer makes print, TV, and radio ads not worth the return on the investment.

There's the dilemma of traditional advertising. Often, the cost outweighs the financial gain and no one is listening anyway because we've been trained since we were born to tune out print ads and commercials.

Telemarketers – They Make Used-Car Salespeople Look Good

However, there's still telemarketing, right? True, but let's be honest here. We all hate telemarketing. It's pretty tough to put your resources into something you yourself don't like. Moreover, so many laws have been passed to regulate the types of calls you can make to whom and when, that the return on the money spent is questionable at best.

If you're in a business-to-business sector, you're in a tough situation. Administrative assistants learned long ago how to keep you from reaching their bosses with your pitch. Like cold calling, telemarketing is considered an interruption. It's not only creating a disruption, it is costing the person on the end of the line time and money. Business people don't want their day taken up by sales pitches. They don't like them and they don't respond to them because they start off on the wrong foot automatically.

Direct Mail Is Called Junk Mail for a Reason

Direct mail has some of the same inherent problems as these other advertising avenues. Of course, that's the nice word for the unsolicited mailings that show up in mailboxes. Most people call it junk mail. Your marketing people can call it anything they want to, but if the person receiving the piece has been trained that unsolicited mail is junk mail, then your direct mail piece is junk mail. There's no way for you to change this perception. It doesn't matter how well conceived your direct mail is. If it ends up in the garbage, it's just well-conceived junk that no one paid attention to.

Websites Don't Get Visited & Believed – Unless It's From a Credible Expert

Websites, on the other hand, are very useful in educating a customer or the public in general. You have plenty of space to work with and adding more pages is easy. While the online medium has plenty of space to get your message across, the challenge is still getting people to visit your website and to believe what appears on it.

Otherwise, a website that nobody sees or believes isn't particularly helpful.

E-mail Gets Lost – Unless It's from Trusted Messengers

E-mails suffer the same problem as traditional direct mail. If it's not expected or solicited, it is perceived as junk mail. In this day and age of spam filters, most people don't even know your e-mail arrives in their inbox to begin with. Certainly, the trust level for an unsolicited e-mail is zero. No one with any smarts is going to click on any link in it, fearing it will lead to malware, a spoof, or Trojan horse.

If your prospects know and trust you, your e-mails get through, get read, and get acted upon. If your prospects don't trust you, it doesn't matter what you write; it won't get considered.

In-Person Sales – "The Chicken or the Egg" Problem

Finally, we've arrived at the standard bearer of all marketing and sales, the face-to-face meeting. It wasn't so long ago that you could walk into a waiting room and see up to a dozen sales people all waiting their turn to see a buyer, executive, or other decision-maker.

With the advent of computers and online buying systems, as well as teleconferencing and even videoconferencing, the face-to-face meeting is becoming harder to get. Rarely will a decision-maker see a salesperson without an appointment and appointments aren't made with just anyone. A person's time is very precious these days, and getting a meeting with someone you've never met or worked with before is difficult.

I personally like face-to-face meetings a lot. It's a quick way to build rapport and establish trust, and you can fully explain your value proposition clearly and succinctly to the person that makes the ultimate decision.

However, getting in-person meetings is a "chicken or the egg" problem. You can't get an appointment without the prospect trusting you or your company, and you can't establish trust without getting a face-to-face meeting.

As you can see, prospects are overwhelmed with advertising, don't trust anyone, and insist on being educated before buying. Sadly, most traditional marketing only adds to the feelings of being overwhelmed, distrust and lack of useful education in the marketplace.

Traditional marketing no longer provides value to prospects so they have come to ignore it. In turn, traditional marketing that gets ignored is of no value to marketers. The traditional marketing model is broken.

To prosper in today's marketplace, a new and different approach is needed.

Section II: Authority In Marketing

CHAPTER 3

The Five Secrets to Marketing in the New World

In the first section, we looked at the five disturbing trends that are affecting traditional marketing, making it extremely difficult to be cost effective and productive.

Let's review them quickly:

1. Advertising overload
2. Widespread skepticism and distrust
3. An educated consumer
4. The messenger rules
5. The importance of substance

What I want to do now is walk you through the major lessons learned if you want marketing to be effective and what you need to do to turn things around in your favor.

Secret #1:
Overcome Advertising Overload by Making Sure Your Advertising Doesn't Look Like Advertising

In a world of advertising overload, if your advertising looks like advertising, you are dead. Perception is reality. If your advertising looks like clutter, it is clutter. To stand out and get noticed, you have to deviate from what your jaded prospects are already used to seeing.

In addition to being different, you must be relevant, too. The combination of offering something relevant and different at the same time is what gets you and your company noticed in a clutter-filled world.

Secret #2:
Establish Trust Before Even Attempting to Sell

You can't trust anyone anymore. That's what your prospects are thinking when they attempt to process the 3,000 advertising messages they see in a day.

In today's world, your marketing must deliberately set out to earn people's trust *first*, before you ever mention your products or services. Otherwise, you're just wasting your time.

Take a look at the marketing from you and your competitors. How much of your industry's marketing is devoted to establishing the trustworthiness of the company vs. promoting a specific product or service? If most of your efforts are product or service centric, you have a problem. Your prospects won't believe what you say.

You need to deliberately establish and prove your trustworthiness before attempting to sell your prospects anything. Until you accomplish the task of establishing trust, none of your sales and marketing makes much of a difference.

Many years ago, I was the interim Chief Information Officer of a high-tech company that is now publicly traded on the NASDAQ stock market. I remember one time I was meeting with a salesperson and he told me something about his product that was blatantly wrong. It was a simple fact that I had learned from the home page of his company's website. I don't know if the guy was lying to me or was simply incompetent, but once I determined he could not be trusted, I literally cut the meeting short on the spot and politely threw him out of my office for wasting my time. There was no way I was going to stake my career on someone I didn't trust. I really didn't care what products and services his company had to offer. If I couldn't trust him, I couldn't do business with him. I doubt I'm alone in this regard.

The big lesson is this: Deliberately work to establish trust *first* (even sacrificing opportunities to talk about your products), *then* you've earned the right to talk about your products and services.

Secret #3:
Win the Battle to Educate Prospects and You Often Automatically Win the Sale, Too

In today's world, customers are looking to educate themselves *before* they compare vendors and buy. If you do not deliberately seek out prospects in "information gathering" mode, then you are vulnerable to a competitor willing to do so.

If you wait until buyers are actively looking to compare vendors before you target them, one day you may find that you were disqualified before you even had a chance to present your case. You may find that you've been pre-empted by a competitor savvy enough to grab all the early prospects for him or herself.

In this "learn first, buy second" environment, it's just common sense if you're the first person to do a fantastic job at educating your prospects on all of their options, your company will end up being the default "go to" provider in the process. If you do a good job at winning the right to educate your prospect first, they won't even bother to look elsewhere.

Most companies still put the vast majority of their focus on prospects that want to "buy right now." What they don't realize is that all of the "must buy now" prospects were "information gathering" prospects a few days or weeks ago. Since very few companies go after the "information gathering" prospects, it's an easy battle to win. In addition, your competitors never realize that you're stealing all of their prospects before they become active comparison shoppers.

By placing the majority of your marketing resources one step earlier in the buyer's purchasing process, you accomplish two things. First, it costs less to target the early-stage prospects because your competitors aren't competing with you for their attention. Second, it's more effective because there is a tremendous shortage of truly useful educational materials that buyers can turn to during the "information gathering" mode.

Secret #4:
Your Marketing Strategy Must Deliberately Make You The Trusted Industry Expert

As I mentioned, this is the age of the messenger. Marketing is no longer just about what is said, but who says it. When you're the obvious expert in your field – trusted, respected, and well known – the more weight your words will carry.

You become the trusted voice of reason and clarity in a sea of confusion. Your staff can piggyback on your status as an authority figure and industry expert to open and close more deals.

Becoming the industry expert requires you to engineer your reputation. This is a deliberate process. It is no longer just good enough to be an expert. You have to possess the symbols of authority. This means that you have to address that point directly in your marketing strategies so that you can become the expert people trust and turn to.

Secret #5:
Substance Matters – Have a Unique Story to Tell and Favor Marketing Methods That Allow You to Tell Your Entire Story

Finally, there's a lesson to be learned from the age of substance, our fifth disturbing trend. More than ever, your company, products, and services must offer unique value. You must be different in a useful and relevant way.

It's nearly impossible to stand out if you do not possess anything that legitimately makes you different.

That being said, just having something that legitimately makes your company different is not enough. You must have a communication vehicle that gives you the room to tell your whole story.

This means that you cannot simply rely on "short form" marketing formats like short television commercials, advertisements, and the like. Somewhere in your marketing system, you must have "long form" communication tools that give you the space and room to tell your whole story.

These five secrets form the foundation of how much you modify your marketing approach in the new world. Prospects are overwhelmed with advertising, don't trust anyone, and insist on being educated before buying. In addition, how prospects receive your sales message depends entirely on whether or not you personally are a trusted and known entity in your field. Finally, prospects want to buy products and services that deliver unique value.

CHAPTER 4

Authority-Based Marketing

With five mega trends impacting how customers buy, it only makes sense that the winners in this new world will exploit these trends, while the losers will insist on ignoring them.

In this new world, there's one approach to marketing that addresses all five of these mega trends. It's something I call "authority-based marketing." This involves adding a piece to your arsenal of marketing weapons that helps you establish your credibility and authority. It solves all the problems that arise from the five mega trends we discussed earlier and often addresses all of these problems in a single shot.

The premise of authority-based marketing is that in our society, obvious experts and authority figures have a significant competitive advantage. Respected authority figures enjoy the opportunity to get attention from others and get their message heard and acted upon more easily than someone who isn't an authority figure.

In a moment, you'll see how deliberately establishing yourself as an authority figure addresses all the secrets to succeeding in the new world. But first, it's useful to understand the psychology behind authority and why possessing authority is enormously powerful.

The Psychology of Authority

When I was an undergraduate and graduate student at Stanford University, I spent a lot of time in the psychology department. While I was there, I came across a truly fascinating piece of research by Stanley Milgram that I've never forgotten.

Back in the 1960's, Milgram did some groundbreaking research surrounding authority figures. It's a bit technical, but if you follow along, I think you'll get something out of it.

Milgram wanted to understand whether authority figures mattered when trying to persuade people to perform a particular activity.

Here's how the experiment worked. He began by telling prospective research subjects that he was conducting an experiment that looked at whether punishing someone for doing something incorrectly would actually improve their performance. It involved three people: a researcher, a student, and a "teacher." After the student answered each question, the researcher would state whether the answer was wrong or right.

If the answer was wrong, the researcher instructed the teacher to penalize the student. The researcher instructed the teacher to press a little button to deliver an electrical shock to the student. It wasn't a real shock, but the teacher didn't know this. Each time the "shock" was administered, the student would pretend to react to it and yell out in pain.

To make the situation more interesting, each time the student gave a wrong answer the strength of the electrical shock delivered was increased. As the test went on, the student's complaints of pain would escalate in response to the supposed increase in electrical current. As the pain level went up, the student would beg the teacher to stop the shocks.

The experiment was meant to see how long the teacher would continue delivering shocks (despite the student begging him or her to stop), simply because the researcher asked him or her to do so.

Finally, the dial was turned up to where a sign warned of impending danger. Around the tenth or twelfth question, the student complained about his heart and the teacher heard a slam as the person supposedly slumped over in the chair and hit the floor. The researcher would continue to tell the teacher to administer more shocks, even as the person supposedly lay unconscious in the next room.

The truly shocking part of the study was that 65% of the people in the study continued to shock the person past the point of the student supposedly collapsing, all because a person who looked like an authority figure told them to.

Obviously, this kind of study created a lot of stress, even when the subject of the study was told what had actually happened afterwards. While this type of study is no longer done today (many of the "teachers" suffered from anxiety problems due to their perception that they may have inadvertently harmed someone), Milgram and his colleagues ended up performing nearly a dozen variations of the experiment to validate the results.

In the role of the "teacher," they put young people, old people, every ethnic group you could think of, educated people, uneducated people, wealthy people, and poor people. The results were consistent across the board. About 65% of the people tested would shock the student to the max. These subjects would obey the person of authority and literally cause (at least in their minds) someone to lose consciousness after complaining of a heart problem.

These results were quite surprising to everyone involved. Most psychologists had anticipated perhaps 1 or 2% of the "teachers" would "shock to the max." Milgram kept experimenting to figure out what factor was causing these teachers to comply so readily.

After many attempts, he found making just one tiny change caused the "teacher" to stop shocking the "student" immediately 100% of the time.

Milgram did a simple role reversal. Without changing any of the words in the pre-written script for the experiment, he simply changed who said what. In this case, rather than have the researcher insist the shocks continue, and the student beg to stop the shocks, he simply flipped it. He had the researcher beg the teacher to stop the shocks, and the student insist the shocks continue. After the first shock, not a single teacher continued to shock.

It's important to keep in mind that in this role-reversal version of the experiment, the information (e.g., the message) delivered to the "teacher" was identical. The only difference is who said it. When the researcher or authority figure said, "Shock the student," the teacher did. When a non-authority figure said the same thing, none of the teachers continued the shocks.

It turns out that Milgram's research shows that when you want to influence someone to do something, what is said is not nearly as important as who is saying it. In short, the identity of the messenger makes a big difference on the outcome of the message itself. Simply put, people say "yes" to people who are authority figures more often than those who are not.

You can see that authority figures have enormous power — power that can be used for good or bad purposes. Of course, I share these powerful lessons with you under the expectation that you will use the power of authority solely for legitimate and ethical purposes. A doctor insisting that a patient take a life-saving medication would be an example of authority at work. A janitor cleaning the hospital floors saying the same thing to the patient is less effective. Authority gets results. The lack of authority produces a lack of results.

Milgram's work showed clearly that by being an authority figure, your chances of being heard, listened to, and acted upon is far greater than if you say the exact same thing without being a perceived authority.

Deliberately Turn Yourself into an Authority Figure

The basis of "authority-based marketing" is to make a deliberate, sustained effort through marketing to establish yourself as an authority figure, one that can be trusted, who's recognized and accepted by others, and whose recommendations are actively considered.

That's the entire premise – turning yourself into an authority figure before you ever buy another ad, produce another brochure, or purchase another listing in the Yellow Pages.

This is a pretty powerful shift in the way to do business. By becoming an authority figure, you'll solve a lot of the problems of the five mega trends that are making traditional marketing less effective each year.

If you recall, these problems include:

1. Advertising overload
2. Widespread customer skepticism and distrust
3. Customers bias towards pre-purchase education
4. The messenger matters more than the message
5. It takes real substance to standout in markets where everyone looks and seems the same

Being an authority figure makes all of your other marketing more effective. It also reduces sales resistance and increases revenue.

Let's look at an example. E-mail is a great vehicle for marketing, if you can get someone to read it. If you're a stranger, chances are good your e-mail will never be opened, let alone read. However, if you're someone whose name is recognized and respected, the e-mail gets opened almost every time. This is not only true for you personally, but your sales team as well. If the company's name is recognized, the recipient is more likely to open it.

The same is true for magazines and newspapers. If you buy advertising space, people won't view you as authoritative or credible because you're obviously selling something. However, if you write an article or are quoted in one, you become an authority, and your message gets considered far more often than if you are just an advertiser.

In the next chapter, we'll look at seven proven ways to turn yourself into a figure of authority.

CHAPTER 5

The Seven Ways to Become an Authority Figure

If you want to establish yourself as a figure of authority, there are seven ways to do it.

Method #1:
Publish a Book

In most parts of the world, published authors are automatically considered experts. I think the weight we give authors has a lot to do with our education. From elementary school through graduate school, we devour textbooks as part of our coursework. For most people, it is hard to change 10 to 15 years of conditioning that books are written by experts who know more than they do.

The simplest way to piggyback on this inherent bias in most people is simple. Publish a book and they automatically assume you're an expert.

Method #2:
Be Quoted in an Article

As noted earlier, members of the media need experts. If you are quoted in a publication about a trend or news item, then you are perceived as an authority on the subject. Note that I said perceived. It doesn't matter what you said or whether it was true or not. The mere fact that you're quoted in a legitimate publication is almost as good as having published a book. It doesn't matter whether it's a national publication or not. If you're quoted in an industry trade publication on a regular basis, or if reporters in smaller sectors quote you as an expert, you are on the road to becoming an authority figure.

Method #3:
Get Articles Written about You and Your Company

Feature articles are a great way to establish your reputation and credibility. A feature article is entirely about you and your company. It's a big public relations victory, and it goes a long way toward establishing your expert status.

For features, reporters seek out those subjects who will make an interesting story and this includes published authors. Of course, everyone in the media checks what their competition is doing. Eventually, as your name keeps popping up repeatedly in the press, more reporters will see you as someone worth interviewing.

Method #4:
Deliver Speeches at Industry Events

As a published author, you will get more speaking engagements more easily. Being recognized as a frequent industry speaker furthers that reputation.

It's important to keep in mind that event promoters don't like taking risks on speakers. They want credible speakers, such as authors, on the agenda. It's a safe choice for them. If they're ever challenged about why they picked you to be on the agenda, they can say it's because you're an expert and author on the topic.

Method #5:
Write and Publish Articles

Writing articles or columns for industry publications is a good way to get you and your company's name out there. If you are the one explaining how to tackle the complex issues your prospects face, then you become the trusted expert in your field – an enviable position indeed. If you're not much of a writer, hire a ghostwriter to write the article itself, and publish it under your own name.

Either way, the simplest way to be an expert is to publish often. A single article is good, and an ongoing series or a column is even better.

Method #6:
Be Interviewed on TV or Radio

When you appear on radio or television, you're

perceived as an expert instantly. How do television reporters and show producers decide who gets to be on a program? They use the same criteria as customers, prospects, and event promoters do. They look for experts and authority figures. Where do they find these experts? They look for people who have a book out, who are being quoted in magazines and newspapers, and who are appearing at a major trade event or conference. They assume these people know what they're talking about.

Method #7: Ensure Your Ideal Prospect Sees All of Your Other Authority-Building Activities

If you've already been quoted in print or broadcast, had a book published, written articles, or have been a featured speaker, get reprints, copies, and recordings of these materials and appearances and send them to your company's top prospects and customers. This demonstrates your company's market leadership to prospects. It reassures your existing customers that they made a great choice and helps to retain them as long-term customers that refer others.

Authority Building in Action

Newspaper and magazine advertising isn't very effective because people are trained to tune it out. However, one type of advertising that works well is an advertisement that looks like an article written by an expert. Simply use your status as an author to write an article-style advertisement.

The reason this works so well is because articles get read three to five times more often than advertisements. When you use your author status to write article-style ads, you benefit from the reader's major preference to read article-style information.

Telemarketing can work the same way. If you're selling something, people don't want to listen. However, if your sales staff offers prospects a free video of your speech at a well-known industry event instead, your team will get better results. They're no longer calling to get a sale. They're calling to offer genuinely useful knowledge with no strings attached. Customers despise the first approach, but they welcome the latter. It's a lot easier to close more sales when your sales team is welcomed rather than despised.

Here's another way to take advantage of these methods. If you've published a book, you can give it away to specifically targeted prospects. You can either have your sales people send it by mail in advance of a telephone or in-person appointment or leave it behind following one. By giving away the book, you're getting people to buy into the fact that you're an expert on the subject matter.

That's a powerful thing. By adding a free book to your sales and marketing process and making sure it gets into the hands of qualified prospects, you can really boost your credibility. This causes prospects to pay more attention to what you and your sales team have to say.

When you are quoted in an article or have a feature written about you or your company, make reprints. Add these to the marketing materials you send out, to your press or sales kit, and put them on your website. Add the verbiage, "As seen in the *New York Times*," or "As seen in the *Wall Street Journal*." You can leverage off their authority by showing that you're in their publication. Being in a major publication is a very effective way to establish credibility.

If you or your staff members are meeting face-to-face with prospects, you want to change the purpose of the meeting from selling to education. The easiest way to do this is to hand the prospective client or customer your book at the beginning of the meeting.

When you do this, suddenly you and your staff are experts sharing information rather than salespeople trying to close a sale. The entire tone of the meeting changes on a dime as a result and puts you and your team in the position of trusted advisers who are interested in helping their business rather than just sucking a dime or two out of their budgets.

As you can see, authority figures and the companies led by authority figures have an easier time getting customers in tough markets.

Of the seven ways to establish yourself as an authority, publishing a book is the "sweet spot" place to start. That's because once you publish a book, it opens up the doors to all the other authority-building activities – publicity, public speaking, article publishing, and media interview opportunities.

If you do nothing else, a book can establish credibility and increase revenues. The media will be much more responsive to you, event promoters will want to book you for speaking engagements, and you'll be invited to appear on television and radio shows if your area of expertise is mass-market oriented. Over time, you'll find yourself being recognized in your industry as an authority. Prospects will seek out you and your company, and when your sales staff contacts them, prospects will be much more likely to pay attention.

Deliberately working on your status as an authority figure in your industry is probably the most useful and under-utilized tool to generate new business. When you're an authority figure, how prospects perceive you changes from chief salesperson of your company to respected industry expert. These positive feelings have a "halo effect" that transfers to your sales staff. Rather than being seen as just another set of salespeople, your salespeople have the opportunity to be perceived as taking on a more consultative role. This happens because they'll be seen as being associated with the industry expert – namely *you*.

CHAPTER 6

The #1 Authority-Building Tool

By now, you should begin to see why publishing a book is such a powerful idea. It cuts through the clutter, establishes you as an expert or authority, and it establishes you as someone others want to do business with.

A book is a symbol of expertise in our society. It's a lot like the scene in the *Wizard of Oz* when the Scarecrow was presented with a diploma as a sign of intelligence. It was nothing more than a symbol of something he already had. A book is the same thing in our world. If you look at television and radio talk shows, they're filled with people who are recognized authorities because they have a book or two under their belts.

The book is the key that unlocks the other six ways to establish and build authority. The seven steps together (if you include publishing a book in the first place) address the five disturbing trends that have made traditional marketing efforts moot.

I referenced these different trends in the beginning. Let's go through each of these and see how publishing a book addresses each trend.

In the age of advertising information overload, a book isn't thought of as advertising. It's education. As a result, the use of a book as part of your marketing arsenal doesn't appear to be an advertisement. It is considered on its own merits and not automatically looked upon with distrust, which leads us to our next point.

In an age of distrust, a book is not automatically viewed with suspicion. We are trained from the time we are first able to read that books are the path to knowledge. We look to books as voices of authority. We study them, we highlight them, and we learn from them. People believe the information in a book to be accurate and true.

When you present a book you wrote to a prospective customer, it carries a lot of weight—certainly more weight than your competitor's sales brochure. If you compare the two side by side, which has more immediate credibility, a book or a sales brochure? The book will win every time.

By giving prospects your book, you show that you are interested in giving them your knowledge without expecting anything in return. In reality, what you and your staff do get (without having to ask for it outright) is an immediately warmer relationship with them. They are much more likely to return your staff's phone calls, to grant them time, and to listen to them.

In an age of distrust, a book builds and accelerates trust instantly.

To Sell More, Educate More Prospects

An educated customer is a customer who's ready to make a purchase. Nearly every buyer does some research about the seemingly most insignificant item these days before he or she buys. The first company to answer the customer's questions and create confidence is the one that will probably get the sale. When you publish a book and get it into the customers' hands during this stage of the game, you are helping them get the answers they are looking for. You and your company become their source of knowledge before the prospects are even aware of your competitors.

As a result, the playing field shifts in your favor. Your role is one of educator, not salesperson. The sales part comes later, of course. By educating, you meet the customer's most important need at the moment. It's like a dance. The prospect wants education. Your book educates them. They get the information they need to make a decision. When they're closer to buying, your team is there to answer their call. The more you are in sync with their needs, the more likely your company will be the one they purchase from.

In the age of the messenger, the messenger is more important than the message. When you publish a book, you become an authority figure. As a trusted messenger, your message carries more weight instantly. People will pay attention to you and your company, even if you're saying the same things you said before you were published.

Let's say you and a competitor are going head to head in the marketplace. He gets the first chance to pitch. The pitch spells out why the prospect should do business with his company, not yours. Then you get your chance.

You introduce yourself as the author of a book that is highly relevant to the prospect, and then you say that you fundamentally disagree with what the previous person said. You then spell out your case, you quote from your book, and you explain your reasons why the first guy was wrong, based on your expertise in the field. Who's going to win this tug of war for business?

It doesn't matter who's right or wrong. You're the published author, you're the authority, and you have all the symbols required to support your position. Your competitor could be right in saying his company is the best for the job, but because he's just a salesperson, not a teacher, he'll get ignored. That's the difference, right there, and it's an important distinction. People will pay attention to an author or teacher, whereas they won't give the time of day to a salesperson.

In an age of substance, it's more important than ever to differentiate your company, products, and services from those of your competitors. Unfortunately, doing this in a 30-second commercial or in a couple of paragraphs of advertising is nearly impossible to do – not to mention expensive. You just can't do an adequate job, except to make sweeping generalizations that "you're better than the other guy." In a book, you have all the room in the world. You have the space needed to explain all the differences as well as provide really useful information.

If prospects read the book, they will see first hand that you are an authority on the subject. If they only glance at the cover of your book, their perception of you instantly shifts from salesperson to industry expert. When you or your salespeople want to make a point, simply quote key ideas from your book. This improves the legitimacy of anything you or your salespeople say and makes it more likely the prospect will respond favorably.

Here's a rule of thumb I find useful. If a customer comes to you and you have 30 to 60 seconds to close the sale, what can you sell them? If they're thirsty or hungry, you can sell a bottle of Coke or a candy bar pretty easily, as their needs can be met quickly with an impulse item. What if you're trying to sell something that's more complex or is a high-ticket item? It's tough to do in that space of time, but that's all the time you have in an advertisement or commercial.

A book is more like a one to three-hour conversation. The information contained in a book can be the equivalent of several face-to-face meetings and a round of questions and answers. In the age of substance, very few vehicles can allow you to convey an entire message like a book can. A website comes close, but it's not linear like a book. Your prospect may get distracted and start clicking around the information you're trying to get across. It also lacks the authority status a book has.

The Psychology of a Sale

Before we get too far into the nuts and bolts of a book, let's look a bit at the psychology of a sale and how a book fits into it. As you know, psychology involves understanding how the human mind works and what human nature is. When a person represents a company, product, or service, it's human nature to automatically assume the individual wants to sell you something. When you're a published author, even if you are a salesperson at heart, prospects suddenly perceive you as an expert. This shifts the dialogue from sales to education.

With a book under your belt, you become a teacher. Your salespeople become "assistant teachers." Whereas your overtures may be rebuffed when you're in sales mode, the time you spend teaching is welcomed and valued. Who is more trusted – a salesperson or a teacher? I don't think that even requires a response here.

Even after all the years of schooling I've been through, I never thought any of my teachers were lying to me or making things up. I always assumed they were telling the truth. When I walk onto the lot of a car dealership, however, my guard is already up. I walk in assuming the salesperson will lie to me. It doesn't mean they really will lie to me, but perception is reality. Many people have the perception that salespeople are not trustworthy.

If you're in sales mode, prospects know you want something from them (money) and will run away from you. When you publish a book and become an authority, people seek you out instead. Even if the ultimate goal is a sale, the tables have turned from one of chasing prospects to drawing them to you. People like to think it was their idea that they want to buy from you.

In a traditional sales cycle, people love to buy but they hate to be sold to. Customers don't like to be pursued by a salesperson because it feels adversarial. Even most salespeople – one-third to one-half in fact – admit that they feel embarrassed to be in the sales profession. Somehow, it doesn't seem as honorable as being a doctor or professor, even though these other professions involve just as much selling (of ideas, for example) as any other.

When you're a published author, and you ensure your prospects know this, something interesting happens. Prospects suddenly become more receptive to you and your company. You don't pursue them; they pursue you and, by proxy, your company. It's a strange shift in the way the process works. Instead of your doing the selling, the customer sells himself or herself on doing business with you and your company.

Earlier, I talked about the importance of building trust in a relationship, particularly in an age of distrust. When you ask for a customer's business before you've proven yourself, why should they trust you? When you provide a prospect with your book, it demonstrates your knowledge and expertise before they even have to make a purchasing decision. This generates enormous trust and opens the door to greater sales for your sales team. They trust you and, by proxy, trust the company you lead and the salespeople you send their way.

The Mrs. Fields "Free Sample" Strategy

When Mrs. Fields first got started, she knew she had a phenomenal product. Once a customer purchased her cookies, they knew it too. The problem was getting a person to taste the cookies in the first place. To solve this problem, she came up with the strategy of giving free samples to people passing by her store.

She went out on the sidewalk in front of her first store and started giving away samples. Customers quickly discovered that her product was indeed amazing and flocked to the store. Because of her "free sample marketing," they knew exactly what they would get for their money before they even reached for their wallets.

I remember the first time I took advantage of a Mrs. Fields free sample. I was busy walking in the mall, in a rush, and had never heard of Mrs. Fields. If they had asked me to buy a cookie, I would have kept walking. I'm busy and have better things to do. However, they didn't ask me to buy a cookie – they offered to give me a free bite of one.

My first reaction was, "Oh, this is unexpected." I had to turn off what I call my "busy person's auto-pilot" and stop and think about what this person just offered me. I was expecting a solicitation that I was planning to automatically decline. But much to my surprise, this wasn't a solicitation. It was a free sample of something that looked (and smelled) quite interesting. The lady with the free sample tray only had to give me a small nudge. She said, "They're really good. It's free."

They got me. I grabbed the free sample and kept on walking. After a few feet of walking, I finally realized, "Wow, this cookie is amazing." I promptly stopped, turned around, and walked back. This was the first time I noticed the Mrs. Fields name. Up until then, I had ignored the name. I ended up buying a bunch of cookies and continue to buy them even decades later.

How to Apply the "Free Sample" Strategy to Your Business

When you publish a book relevant to your prospect's situation, it provides him or her with a free sample of your expertise.

Done properly, your prospect's reaction will be, "Wow, that was so useful and clear." Their next reaction will be, "Who is this author again? What company does he or she lead? How do I reach them to take the next step?" They will shift towards seeking you out. In short, they start paying attention to you and your company, whereas before they didn't even notice you and certainly wouldn't give you or your company the time of day.

When you're selling a high dollar item or something that's very complex, the education provided by your book reduces sales resistance and brings the prospect to a purchasing decision more quickly. They don't have to risk a penny in the process.

They become highly educated prospects that are enthusiastic about you and what your company has to offer. When they're ready to buy, they're more likely to buy from you and your company because you're a known entity. They perceive that doing business with you is much safer than doing business with someone else who has not taken the trouble to establish trust and authority first.

Let's recap for a moment. Publishing a book accomplishes several important things in establishing your authority. First, it allows you to reach a larger audience – an audience that's more likely to listen to an obvious expert than a salesperson. Second, it reverses the dynamic of salesperson chasing the prospect. By becoming an expert, you invite prospects to seek you and your company out. In cases where you still need to nudge prospects a little, they are much more likely to treat you and your sales team like peers than the people who are wasting their time.

Finally, if you sell high-ticket products and services, publishing a book allows you to create a "free sample" entry point into your business. Once they're willing to make a small commitment toward your business, it's much easier to get them excited to take advantage of your more expensive offerings.

Section III:
The Bookmercial As A Marketing Tool

CHAPTER 7

The Bookmercial

Books can take many forms, but the most effective format I have found to address all the opportunities available today is what I call the Bookmercial. The Bookmercial is similar to an infomercial you see on television. It is half book and half commercial for your business.

To make this style of book work well, you must weave together seamlessly the book portion and the commercial portion. You want it to be tough to tell where the education stops and the advertising takes over. This is one of the reasons why the Bookmercial is so effective. Customers can readily see the value of the information presented, while they also happen to learn more about your company's products and services.

The "Sweet Spot" for a Bookmercial

A Bookmercial is not appropriate for every type of business. If your company sells low-ticket products that are easily understood by customers, you'll find other marketing tools will more than meet your needs. For example, a Bookmercial does not make sense as a way to sell Coke, Tide, or Ivory Soap.

In addition, a Bookmercial is generally not useful when the customer sees the purchasing decision as low risk and easily reversible. In these situations, the purchase is a "low involvement" decision where the buyer does not want to be actively engaged in the purchase.

For example, for most people, buying toilet paper is a "low involvement" decision. If they make a bad decision, they can always return it or buy something different next time. Most people don't feel the need to do much research because the time involved in the research is more trouble than it is worth.

A Bookmercial starts becoming useful as the price, importance, and complexity of the purchase increases. On the consumer side, a financial planning service involving complex life insurance, asset protection techniques, and multiple investments involving one's life savings would be a carefully considered decision typically.

In the business-to-business world, major technology investments or outsourcing decisions are often mission-critical decisions, where the buyer feels the need to do his or her homework, before making such a big decision.

In addition, a Bookmercial is also useful when markets change quickly, vendors say contradictory things, and customers are generally confused. As I mentioned earlier, confused customers do not buy. They just sit there frozen, like a deer in headlights. A Bookmercial helps to demystify the confusion, clarify any myths, and helps the prospect make sense of a confusing marketplace.

Finally, a Bookmercial is useful when the decision-making process involves multiple decision-makers. This is most common in business-to-business situations where a major purchase needs to be approved by multiple decision-makers within an organization. In these situations, a lot of the "selling" takes place behind the scenes between these decisions-makers – typically, without the involvement of vendors. It's a situation where the marketing department favors one vendor, the technology department another, and the finance department a third.

In these situations, you may only have one of the decision-makers who favors doing business with your company. You're essentially counting on your "champion" within the organization to convince his or her peers to favor your company, too. This is a tough situation because your contacts may not be great at convincing others to follow their recommendations.

However, if you have a Bookmercial, you can provide that champion with multiple copies of the book to share with colleagues. In these closed-door meetings, you and your sales team will not be able to get a seat at the table, but your Bookmercial could easily make it into the room. It can be the subject of conversation or used as a reference guide to settle disagreements between peers. It's a way to get you, your company, and your ideas to penetrate deeply within a prospect's organization.

Your Bookmercial can reach more people within a prospect's organization than even the most diligent salesperson ever could.

The Two Objectives of a Bookmercial

A Bookmercial has two primary objectives. The first goal is to reach more prospects. The second is to convert more prospects into buyers.

When you can accomplish these two things, revenue automatically grows in your business. Let's look at each of these areas and see how a Bookmercial contributes to the process.

How to Get More Prospects with a Bookmercial

First, let's talk about how a Bookmercial can help you reach more prospects. By becoming an authority figure, you elevate your status. It opens more doors to free publicity, which in turn allows you to become a speaker at events, be quoted in publications, publish articles, and become recognized as the "go to" person in your field or industry.

Second, you can blend your newfound status as an authority figure and your book into your existing marketing programs. For example, you can include the fact that you're a published author on your website and in your brochures and press releases. Just by adding this simple notation, you can increase the effectiveness of marketing pieces that may have only been marginally effective before.

Through the systematic application of these two techniques, you want your prospects to know of you before they ever know they need you. You want them to have heard or read about you, you want them to have seen your book or even read it, and you want to make sure that it becomes an integral part of your sales process.

Why does this work so well? As I mentioned, buyers fall into two basic categories. There are those who are in the learning mode and those who are in the buying mode. Your competitors are all going after the buyers. It's a blood bath and the sharks are all over the place, trying to go after the same pool of prospects. This is the land of endless proposals that go nowhere when you're one of a dozen companies responding to a "request for proposal." In these situations, you're just one of many lined up for a massive comparison-shopping exercise.

Pre-Emptive Marketing

There's an often-ignored opportunity to circumvent and, in some cases, even prevent this comparison-shopping exercise from happening. This involves targeting prospects earlier in their buying process – while they are still in learning mode. This is where you have enormous influence on the decision-making process.

This pre-emptive marketing strategy is quite powerful. It allows you to channel many of the early-stage buyers to consider your company first, before anyone else. It's the equivalent of rerouting the roads in your town so that every Wal-Mart customer must drive through the Target parking lot first. It's an enviable position, don't you think?

If you're running the Target store, you won't get every one of the Wal-Mart customers to stop, but you'll certainly get more than you did before. A Bookmercial that is targeted to early-stage prospects does the same thing for your company. It gets you in the door before the customer has had a chance to engage your competition. You won't get all of them, of course, but if you're first in line, you do get a fair number of them.

Why Pre-Emptive Marketing Works

When it comes time for customers to make a major, complex purchase, here is the psychology that goes through their mind. Fundamentally, the customer does not know what he or she needs to know. When this happens, he does not buy. He may not be able to articulate this fact if asked, but he will feel hesitant and resist buying because something is not quite right.

What's happening is the customer does not yet trust himself to make a wise decision. At some level, the customer is uncertain that he has the right information or perspective to make a wise choice, so he does not buy.

However, when you're the first company in the door that makes a deliberate effort to establish trust, one of two things happens.

First, it's possible the prospect is so impressed with your knowledge and expertise he starts to trust you more than he trusts himself. An example of this is how most people treat their doctor. The patient may know he's sick, but may not know why or how to fix it. The patient doesn't know what to do so he goes to the doctor. Once there, he is relieved when it's clear the doctor has seen this situation a few dozen times. He does what the doctor says because he trusts the doctor more than he trusts himself to make the right decision.

The other possibility is that the prospect sees you as a useful educational resource. He doesn't trust you to make the buying decision for him, but he does trust you enough to learn from you. Once he learns enough, he suddenly feels like he understands all the major issues, tradeoffs, and pitfalls. This allows him to feel comfortable in trusting his own judgment since he's now so well informed. In this situation, the first company he looks to is almost always the company that provided the most value to him during his information-gathering efforts.

In both situations, your company is the first company considered by the prospect. When you reach out to prospects early in the process and do a good job of educating them, you carve out the position of being the default provider that they consider first. Will you get all of them as customers? No. Do you dramatically increase your odds of getting more customers overall by being the first company they consider? Yes.

How to Use a Bookmercial to Convert Prospects into Customers

Converting more prospects into buyers is the second way a Bookmercial can help you. Confused customers never buy. They don't buy from you; they don't buy from anyone because they're totally confused. A Bookmercial really helps clarify relevant issues, answers questions, explains options, and positions you as the expert on the matter at hand. A Bookmercial also gets your name out there as an authority figure, so the prospect at least knows of you and knows you're knowledgeable enough and respected enough to be published. This alone can get your company's foot in a door that was previously closed.

This has to be done subtly. A Bookmercial is a soft sell. It has to have genuine educational value, because it's the educational content that gets the Bookmercial discussed and passed along within a prospect's organization. The educational content convinces prospects that they need to solve their problem and buy a solution.

A Bookmercial also has to explain why the prospect should do business with your company. While the educational content gets the prospect to buy, the persuasive sales content explains why the customer should buy from you.

One of the reasons a Bookmercial converts more prospects to buyers is because it interweaves educational information with sales information. In actual practice, you don't write the two separately; you carefully choreograph the messages so you can't tell them apart. Let's talk about each individually before we look at how they work together.

Educational Content Garners Readership

The educational component is essential to the success of your Bookmercial. Without it, your prospects are just receiving an ordinary sales piece. The educational content is what creates value for the prospect. You get higher readership and build trust because you're giving them information that helps them make a purchasing decision.

When buyers are in the learning mode, they are receptive to new ideas. You know this already, of course. In school, we all were in a learning mode. We took notes, listened intently, and absorbed information like a sponge. This was just as true with books as it was with teachers. Even as adults, we continue to accept pretty much at face value information that is presented to us when we're in learning mode.

Note that this trust in printed materials does not extend to sales pieces. As soon as we begin to read a sales piece, our defensive measures kick in. Immediately, we wonder if the offer is too good to be true, if the service or product will perform as promised, and whether the company is really on the up and up. We've heard it all before. Worse, we've been burned before.

When we read a book, however, we're more open to the information, even if it runs counter to what we think we already know. To make sure the information you're presenting is internalized, you weave your sales message in with the educational information. When the person is learning, he or she doesn't filter out the subtle sales message, but simply rolls it in with the education.

This doesn't happen with a sales brochure. Prospects don't expect useful information to be in it. They know you want to sell them something, so they're going to gloss over any real information presented, thinking it is just propaganda anyway. If you brag too much, prospects will simply dismiss all the information and throw it in the trash. They can't trust anything you say, even it if is true, because you're trying to sell them something. Sales materials aren't objective. They're all about the "buy" instead of the "why."

The trick is to get past these hurdles. This means you have to have useful information that readers find valuable—so much so that they want to contact you, the authority figure, for more information or to establish a business relationship with your company.

If you have a Bookmercial entitled *The Seven Key Things to Know When Switching to Green Energy*, *The IT Buyers Guide to Network Security Devices*, or whatever, you can use it in a variety of situations. The reason you need the educational content in there is because you must deliver on the promise of providing useful information. This does several things—it gets the book read, it gets your message across, and it causes the prospect to have an open mind.

The sales component of the Bookmercial is equally important. It's the real reason you're sending the book out in the first place. Woven into the educational side, you want readers to understand why they should do business with you. This is why a Bookmercial is very different from a book that only educates customers without persuading them.

A Bookmercial isn't written as much as engineered and choreographed. It is as much science as it is art. It's a very deliberate process, and there are very few people who know how to do this. It takes a lot of skill to provide useful educational material while still selling without appearing to be selling.

Why a Bookmercial Outperforms a Brochure

Before we go much further, let me explain why a Bookmercial is more effective than a traditional sales brochure.

First, a Bookmercial has the room to present a lot of in-depth content that a sales brochure can't. It allows you to tell your unique story and differentiate in great detail your company from the rest of the marketplace. A brochure is often too short to explore any substantive issues that go into the decision-making process.

Second, unlike the typical brochure that's selling from the get-go, a Bookmercial takes a more neutral tone. A neutral tone is perceived as more objective and information presented in this way is believed more often. You provide all the background information that a prospect would need to understand to even begin the process of selecting a vendor.

In addition, instead of just saying your products are the best in the world and are always the best choice, you need to explain all the options available to a customer. One especially powerful technique is to explain why or when a prospect should *not* do business with your company. Most prospects find this unexpected and disarming, as you certainly would never find such information in a brochure.

This accomplishes several things. It deepens their trust in what you have to say and it also causes them to believe you when you explain what kinds of customers should do business with your company.

Third, a well-crafted Bookmercial leads the prospect through a tough decision-making process that ends with him or her buying from your company. A Bookmercial has a consultative look, feel, and substance to it that a typical brochure does not. It's why a Bookmercial gets read more often, gets acted upon, and confers a "halo effect" to you and your staff for being associated with it. It also allows your sales team to continue the consultative sales approach, holding prospects' hands as they walk them through everything they need to know about their situation, problems, and options.

Why a Bookmercial Outperforms a Traditional Book

By now, you've seen how a Bookmercial provides numerous advantages over many forms of traditional marketing. Now let me explain the difference between a Bookmercial and a traditional book.

A book helps prospects to understand and appreciate their problems and often motivates them to solve their problems. A Bookmercial does the same thing, but takes it one step further. It also explains why prospects should buy from your company.

When you publish a book about your industry, you end up promoting your industry. When you publish a Bookmercial, you channel that interest in your industry towards your company.

Let me use this book as an example. You may have been wondering if this book is, in fact, a Bookmercial. It is. You may have also noticed that thus far in this

Bookmercial I have yet to suggest you buy anything from my company. This is deliberate. Let me explain what's going on and, more importantly, why.

First, nobody buys from someone they do not trust. All of the early parts of this Bookmercial have been designed to provide you with useful information about a topic you are interested in – getting more customers in a tough market environment. This builds trust and earns me the right to continue to share information with you.

Second, prospects listen to and act upon the advice of authority figures (but *not* sales people). The early parts of this book have gone to great lengths to explain new ideas to you that impact your business – many of which you may not have realized the importance of previously. This works to establish me as a knowledgeable expert and authority figure. Not to worry – at some point in this Bookmercial I will recommend that you contact my office to take the next step in my sales process. However, if I ask you to do this too early, I come across like a salesperson – a person who routinely gets ignored. Therefore, I'm "investing" words, if you will, in establishing my authority with you.

Third, I know that customers do not buy solutions to problems they don't have, don't know they have, or don't think are urgent. That is why I spent the early part of the book explaining the five trends that diminish the effectiveness of traditional marketing. I did so to ensure that you fully understood the problems facing your company. Until you fully appreciate the problems facing your company, it's a waste of effort to promote products and services to solve a problem you don't even think you have.

The strategy is to "sell" the problem first, then "sell" your industry or product category as a solution to that problem, and, finally, "sell" your company as an ideal choice for a particular type of customer and customer situation. You'll see the rest of this Bookmercial unfold in this way.

Finally, there is a certain belief system that I need you to believe in before you will ever consider buying from my company (as there are certain belief systems that your prospects must adopt or they will not buy from you). Here are two examples.

One is the idea that people who are authority figures have an easier time getting attention from prospects and getting prospects to act on their ideas.

Second is the idea that publishing a book is one of the best, if not the best, symbols of one's status as an authority figure. These two ideas ultimately form the foundation of my sales argument. If you don't buy into these two ideas, there is no way you will ever buy.

On the one hand, these two ideas are useful for you to know, whether or not you do business with me. So, in that respect, my explaining these topics is educational in nature. You can use these ideas in your own business without ever having to do business with my company.

On the other hand, these two ideas also form the foundation of a sales argument I will be making later in this Bookmercial. So, in some respects, I'm "setting up" a future sales argument by addressing these two topics early in my Bookmercial.

Were the chapters on those topics educational or sales-oriented? The answer is: Both. The same is true for every page of this Bookmercial. Each chapter and example is deliberately chosen to both educate and "further the sale" in a way that may or may not be obvious to the casual observer.

Outside of this "sneak peak behind the curtain," I have yet to talk about any specific products or services my company offers. I have also yet to suggest you do business with my company. Make no mistake about it; everything you have been reading so far has been a deliberate effort to "further the sale." I'm simply using this to lay a foundation that I know is a prerequisite before any actual product or service presentation.

The fact that the information also happens to be useful to you in its own right is one of the reasons why the Bookmercial format is effective – you, as the reader, are deriving value from this Bookmercial even while you're learning more about me and my company.

Let's wrap up this behind-the-scenes tour as we head into the next section of this "book." Read on to learn the mechanism behind how you can use a Bookmercial to get publicity, attract leads, and close more sales.

CHAPTER 8

How to Generate Publicity

A Bookmercial is not only a good lead generator; it's also a good way to get coverage in the media. The more you understand how a reporter, talk show host, or show producer thinks, the better chance you have of getting free publicity for your company.

The media is interested in three things.

The first is readership or ratings. Newspaper and magazine reporters care most about what their readers will read. It has to be interesting and relevant to the readers. Readers add up to readership, which adds up to advertising dollars. The same is true for television and radio, only these outlets refer to it in terms of ratings. If no one tunes in, advertisers don't buy advertising and there's no money coming in. At the end of the day, the people who run these media outlets and the people who work for them care about one thing: getting the maximum number of people possible to read, listen, or watch.

Second, competition is fierce, so there's a constant need to provide readers, viewers, and listeners with new content that's interesting and informative. Every morning when reporters wake up, they know they need to fill their pages and minutes with content. They constantly look out for things to write about and to put on the air. The more you can help them do this, the more popular you are with reporters and producers.

Finally, reporters and producers like to look good, especially to their readers and bosses. More important than looking good, they are scared to death of looking foolish. For a reporter, the only kind of expert worth quoting is one that looks like an obvious expert. A published author is the kind of obvious expert that reporters like to rely on. For the reporter, it's simply a form of job security because if there's ever a problem with your quote, they can simply fall back on the fact that you're a published author. Having been quoted in the media several times, I can tell you that being a published author is an instant credibility builder with the media.

Let's look at a few ways to use your Bookmercial to get publicity, attract prospects, and close more sales.

Generate Publicity by Providing Expert Quotes

If you read newspapers, magazines, and trade publications carefully, you'll notice that most of the articles include quotes from relevant experts. This happens for a reason. Without expert quotes, news articles would look like opinion pieces that belong in the opinion and editorial section of the publication instead of the news section. Expert opinions provide justification for the reporter's interpretation of the day's news. Is the news important or not? Is it a big deal or a small deal? Should readers take action in response to the news or just monitor its progress? These are the questions many articles seek to answer. Providing readers with quotes from experts that explain the relevance and implication of the day's news is how these questions are answered. It's an essential part of the process for reporters.

In short, journalists need experts to provide commentary on the day's news. They need experts like you every single day.

The first Bookmercial I produced was for one of my own businesses. Within just 21 days of publication, I was quoted in two business publications. I did not send out a press release. I did not call them. The reporters simply put out a request for experts on topics that I happen to know well, and I responded to their request. It was quite easy. My name, Bookmercial title, and company name were published in their next publication.

It's important to keep in mind that these reporters are under enormous deadline pressure. One reporter who interviewed me had less than six hours to finish her story and desperately needed a quote from me. I saved her day. I was an expert in fact and in perception. I had something interesting to say. I was able to get my comments to her before her deadline. I got published.

The great thing is the next day the reporter is going to be in the exact same situation – under tight deadline pressure, desperately looking for an obvious expert to provide a quote before her deadline.

While I continue to respond to such inquiries, I must admit that even I was surprised at what a dramatic difference being an author had in dealing with the media. The day before adding "author" next to my credentials, in the eyes of the media, I was a "nobody." The day after, I was suddenly a "quotable" expert. While my actual level of expertise did not change in those 24 hours, the media's perception of me changed quite dramatically overnight. In a world where perception is reality, being a published author matters a lot.

Publicity from Trend Stories

The second way to gain publicity is through a trend story. New trends develop all the time, and they are often worthy of media coverage. When reporters do a story on a trend, they're looking for people who will give them more information about the trend and its impact on an industry, the public, or society. For instance, "going green" is a big trend right now, and anything that has to do with slowing global warming – whether it's a new power source or just changes in the way people recycle and reuse – is big news these days. Following the trends, and being able to provide perspective, is a quick way to get publicity for you and your business.

Publicity from Feature Stories

Features are good for your business, too. A feature story is not news. It has a softer approach to the subject and usually focuses on a person, a business that's doing interesting things, or a person who has been in the news recently. Of course, authors are always interesting, particularly if they are writing about subjects that have been in the news lately. Feature writers often follow what their competitors are doing. If you're featured in one publication, don't be surprised if other reporters end up calling as well to put a different spin on the same story.

How to Turn Publicity into Revenues

Publicity gets converted to revenues in two key ways. First, when prospects see your name in print related to a topic they're interested in, they will seek you out. Here's how this works. I advise authors to introduce themselves to the media using the following formula: "My name is John Doe. I'm the author of the book XYZ and the CEO of ABC Company." These three pieces of information are important.

Reporters need your name or they can't quote you. The book title is meant to establish your authority and give prospects a way to realize that your area of expertise is relevant to them. Finally, you mention your company name because it gives the prospects a way to take their interest to the next level.

When you do this, here's how reporters will use it. They'll say something like this: "John Doe, author of the book XYZ and CEO of ABC Company, a leading application service provider, says, 'The reasons customers prefer to purchase their software as a service, rather than buy it outright, is because it dramatically reduces upfront investment. In addition, it forces vendors to keep customers happy each and every month. Overall, it's a great option for customers.'"

Second, you want to guarantee that your prospects see you and your company's name in these publications. The simplest way to do this is just to send them a copy of whatever media coverage you obtain. Get reprints and audio/video clips of all your media mentions and mail them to your prospects. Post them on your website. Hang them on the walls in the lobby of your company's office. Put them in a binder in the waiting area. Change the on-hold music for your phone system to play recordings of your media interviews.

Even most professional public relations professionals fail to take this last step. It's highly effective because your appearance in a publication does a far better job of establishing your company's expertise than you ever could do on your own. The problem with traditional publicity is that your prospects may not read the publication on the day you're quoted. This is an easy problem to solve. Simply get a copy of the article and send it to the prospects you want to influence. It's very effective and furthers the sales process.

CHAPTER 9

How to Obtain Public Speaking Opportunities

Event organizers make money by getting attendees to come to their events. From the attendee's standpoint, the main reason they attend events is to learn from credible speakers about topics they find interesting and relevant.

The key to getting more speaking engagements at industry events is to identify yourself as a published author, and offer to talk about a topic that's relevant to event attendees.

For example, within 20 days of publishing a recent Bookmercial for one facet of my business, I was invited to be a speaker at Harvard Business School, MIT Sloan School of Business, and The Wharton School. This was quite an honor, considering the other business luminaries that have spoken at these institutions in the past include Warren Buffet, Jack Welch, and, quite literally, over a dozen Fortune 500 CEOs each year.

The effort required was surprisingly easy. I simply sent a one-page letter to certain event planners at these institutions. In the letter, I introduced myself as the author of a book relevant to their audience along with my other credentials. Next, I suggested an intriguing topic that might be appropriate for their next event and asked them to contact me if they were interested.

The only times I've run into problems doing this is if I sent the letter to the wrong person or there was a scheduling conflict. Other than that, three out of four attempts have resulted in a speaking invitation. After all, these event planners are under constant pressure to bring interesting topics to their audiences. If you suggest a compelling topic and introduce yourself as a published author and expert, it's easy for them to say, "yes" to you.

It's also worth noting that I am fairly certain that if I were not a published author, there's not a chance Harvard Business School would have invited me to speak.

You'll find that once you get the ball rolling on public speaking, the momentum builds. Initially, the Stanford Graduate School of Business had only moderate interest in inviting me to speak. However, once they heard that I spoke at Harvard, they suddenly became more interested.

Now whenever I introduce myself to media, I add two credentials next to my name. I reference the fact that I'm an author of a book relevant to the article they're working on, and I mention (quite deliberately, I might add) that I've been a speaker at Harvard Business School along with people like Warren Buffet and Jack Welch.

When I'm looking for speaking opportunities at other events, I naturally mention the same thing, and I mention all the publications I've been mentioned in.

You can see there is a natural momentum to turning one's self into a highly recognized authority figure. Speaking opportunities attract media attention. Media attention attracts speaking opportunities. Keep the process up and, in a short while, your market's perception of your expert status grows tremendously.

There's an interesting saying that's relevant to this topic: "He (or she) who gets the most time at the microphone often wins." This occurs for a few reasons. First, if your market is busy paying attention to you, they also happen to be ignoring your competition. Second, anytime you speak or are mentioned in a publication, you implicitly get to "borrow" their credibility and brand recognition and attach it to your name. So I'm no longer just Victor Cheng. Now I'm Victor Cheng, author and former speaker at Harvard Business School. The latter introduction has a bit more power behind it, don't you think?

I've found that my Bookmercial has opened doors to speaking opportunities that were simply closed to me previously. The speaking, in turn, has opened doors to me to media, prospects, and partners that would not have otherwise given my company or me the time of day. It's important to realize that it's not just about the Bookmercial; it's about what you do with it that really matters. In many respects, the publication of my Bookmercial was the initial trigger I needed to jumpstart my efforts to build myself into an authority figure in my industry.

CHAPTER 10

How to Generate Leads

Once you have a Bookmercial published, you can generate leads more readily than you can with any other form of marketing. You can do this in three ways. I'll touch on each one, so you can see how each approach can be used in your own business.

Generate Leads from Publicity

The first source of leads comes from your publicity. These leads are solid because prospects discovered you on their own by reading your book, seeing your name in print, or hearing about you through TV or radio.

In essence, the publication or media outlet endorsed you in the mind of a prospect. As a result, he or she is more open to doing business with you right from the start because the media wrote about you.

Generate Leads by Selling Your Bookmercial

The second way to generate leads is to sell your Bookmercial through online and offline bookstores. Setting this up is a pretty easy process, and it's a very effective marketing tool. For example, you can sell your Bookmercial on Amazon.com and Barnes & Noble through their website. They not only handle all the payments for you, but also allow you to tap into their proven e-commerce and marketing tools.

There are two reasons to make your Bookmercial available for sale in online bookstores – particularly Amazon.com and BN.com (the online bookstore for Barnes & Noble).

The first reason is credibility. When your Bookmercial appears alongside the books of well-known authors, your credibility goes up significantly. A book buyer can buy books by Al Gore, Tom Brokaw, and you. This puts you in a good light.

The second reason is anytime you are quoted in the media, you will typically get more people searching for your company on the Internet and looking for your book at the major online bookstores. Of course, they can only buy your book if it's available for sale.

Generally, you'll find that the kind of person who goes out of his or her way to buy a book online is very interested in your topic. These kinds of people make good prospects.

Another option, with some tradeoffs, is having your book available for sale in brick and mortar bookstores. If your area of expertise is mass-market oriented, traditional bookstores are a good channel. If your topic is too specialized, it generally won't be worth the effort.

Here's why. Big publishing houses like Random House, Warner Books, and McGraw-Hill are the primary ways to get distribution to brick and mortar bookstores. They employ large sales forces to call on the wholesale buyers of these bookstore chains, and they typically promise large-unit sales. If the books do not sell well in the stores within the first 90 days, all of the remaining books are automatically returned to the publisher and refunded. In this case, the book moves from being actively for sale to "remaindered" (meaning sent back for refunds) to "out of print," all in less than four months.

This is the reason, from time to time, you'll stumble upon a fantastic book that is simply no longer for sale. The traditional book publishing and selling process forces books to go out of print if sales don't hit a critical mass within the first 90 days. They do this for financial reasons. Barnes & Noble operates 700 bookstores. If they carry two copies in each store, that's 1,400 books taking up shelf space that can no longer be used to sell a more mass-market oriented title. It's a zero sum game. There is only so much shelf space available, so the space goes to books with the broadest appeal.

For most of the companies considering a Bookmercial, their topic is often quite specialized and unlikely to hit that critical mass level of sales – especially in 90 days. When you consider it takes 12 to 24 months to get a book into bookstores through a traditional book publisher for just 3 months of exposure, it's often not a good tradeoff.

In contrast, online bookstores have unlimited virtual shelf space. Selling your Bookmercial does not interfere with selling mass-market titles. They can do both easily and profitably. In addition, each online bookstore has only one store. They don't need to stock 1,400 titles to get started. Often, they'll start with just two copies provided to them on consignment. Once sales increase, they'll expand their inventory to the purchasing patterns of their buyers. This means the online bookstore has absolutely no downside to selling your Bookmercial. Online bookstores are happy to carry your Bookmercial indefinitely.

For these reasons, online bookstores remain the preferred distribution channel for selling a Bookmercial.

Generate Referrals from Bookmercial Pass-Along

Another way to generate leads from your Bookmercial is through referrals. Normally, when customers of yours refer someone to your company, they might mention your company's name to a friend or colleague. Typically what happens is the person forgets your company name or forgets to follow up. For every one referral you get, it's quite possible there are two or three "almost referrals" that you didn't get due to miscommunication or procrastination.

When you have a Bookmercial at your disposal, here's what you do instead. Rather than have your best customers refer prospects to your company by passing along your company name, teach them to pass along your Bookmercial instead.

First, there is a physical reminder of who you are and what your company can do that's hard to ignore. Most people are hesitant to throw away a book – it just seems too valuable.

Second, your company's contact info is printed in the book, so there's nothing for your new prospect to write down and no lost scraps of paper to dig up.

Third, the new prospect's initial impression of your company goes way up with a Bookmercial, especially one that has been endorsed by a friend or colleague.

And fourth, for the very eager prospect, he or she will start reading your Bookmercial, allowing the sales process to begin well in advance of the prospect even contacting your company. By the time the prospect contacts your company, he or she could easily be 50 to 80% "sold" on doing business with you. These prospects are much easier to close than prospects starting your sales process from the starting line.

One of the things I do now is anytime I send a Bookmercial to a friendly audience (e.g., business partners, referral sources, friends, or clients), I always send two copies of my Bookmercial instead of just one. I always tell them one copy is for them and the other is for a friend or colleague.

Often, the postage is the same, so the incremental cost is minimal. In addition, since the products and services my various businesses sell are high-ticket, I don't need this strategy to pay off very often to make it worthwhile.

Giveaway Your Bookmercial Away for Free to Qualified Prospects

The third and most effective way to generate leads is by using "lead generation advertising" to give your Bookmercial away to qualified prospects. To understand how to use this technique and, more importantly, how to do it correctly, you'll need to understand the various types of advertising options available to you.

The three main types of advertising are: image advertising, one-step advertising, and lead generation advertising (also known as two-step advertising). Let's look at each one.

Image Advertising

The goal of an image advertisement is to get your name out there. You're just trying to get your name known so your prospects will hopefully have heard of you before you contact them. If you are Coke or McDonald's, image advertising can be effective. The best time to use image advertising is when your company or brand is extremely well known in your industry and you simply need to remind previous customers that already love your products that it's time to buy again.

Image advertising tends to be less effective when marketing to an audience that is not familiar with your company. Due to the limited space available, it's difficult to make your case as to why the prospect should buy from your company and not someone else.

In addition, image advertising is often terribly inefficient. Here's why. Image advertisements can only "get your name out there," without actually asking the prospect to take the next step in your sales process – especially a step that you can track. Without the ability to track the effectiveness of an image advertisement, you can't tell if the advertisement is working or not working. This typically means you're spending your marketing dollars blindly, without any ability to make adjustments to your campaign.

For this reason, image advertising is one of the least effective ways to generate leads.

One-Step Advertising

A one-step ad introduces your company, explains your product or service, and asks the customer to make a buying decision right there on the spot. If you open up a *USA Today*, you'll often see one-step advertisements for everything from gold coins and cubic zirconium diamonds to weight loss programs. These are often full-page newspaper ads with either an order coupon at the end of the ad or an 800 number to place an order.

The purpose of this ad is to generate an immediate sale. It works very well for impulse items, particularly low-cost ones. If you can sell a product or service to your customer face-to-face in less than ten minutes, then this type of ad may work for you.

In general, though, it's hard to get a one-step ad to work effectively because of the cost involved. To make the equivalent of a ten-minute sales presentation in a newspaper ad, you need a large ad. Large ads are expensive. To run a full-page ad just once in *USA Today* costs well over $100,000.

Another problem is you have no second or third chance to sell to the people who were interested in your offer but did not happen to buy. There's no opportunity to send them more information or to call them to follow up.

Finally, many complex and high-ticket products and services simply cannot be sold in less than 10 minutes. Often, these are much more complicated decisions, where it's impossible for any reasonable buyer to make a decision with just 10 minutes worth of information.

For these reasons, one-step advertising is not a cost-effective choice for generating leads.

Lead Generation (or Two-Step) Advertising

Unlike the other two forms of advertising, lead generation advertising carries a lower risk, is more controllable, and is easier to improve upon over time.

Rather than trying to sell your product in just one step in the initial advertisement, the two-step approach splits the sales process into two steps. The first step is a lead generation advertisement that offers prospects something that is free and useful in exchange for providing you with their contact information. The second step is to follow up with those interested prospects, send them a useful information kit (typically your Bookmercial), and, ultimately, sell them your product or service.

There are several benefits to splitting this process into two steps. First, when you're selling something that's free, it takes a whole lot less advertising space to get the job done. As a result, the size of your ads and advertising budget can be much smaller.

Second, lead generation advertising is one of the fastest low-cost ways of building a database of interested prospects. Because the free offer is so enticing, the number of leads you capture goes up substantially. Often, a free offer will capture two to five times more leads than an offer that costs even a small amount of money. In other words, you'll get two to five times as many people to request your free Bookmercial than you will to buy it for $19.95.

This free offer approach works best under the following conditions: 1) your company sells high-ticket products and services, and the revenue potential of each lead is worth more than $19.95; and 2) your advertisements run in highly targeted publications where the vast majority of readers are people you want to be your customers (this reduces the risk of unqualified "freebie seekers" responding to your free offer).

The Basics of Lead Generation Advertising

Lead generation advertising also allows you to establish your credentials without going into sales mode. By giving your book to prospects for free, you not only demonstrate your expertise, but also your willingness to help educate them rather than just making a quick buck from a sale. Perhaps just as important, you gain important contact information for a follow-up call or e-mail, establishing a permission-based relationship.

There are two different formats for lead generation advertisements – the short version and the long version.

Short Version Lead Generation Advertisement

The short version has a headline, a free offer, and a way for the prospect to request the free offer, such as a website address or phone number.

For example, the headline may be: "How to Tackle the Growing Spam Problem in Large Companies." The body copy says, "Get a free, recently published book on the seven key ways to eliminate spam in large companies. To request a copy of this free book, call (800) 555-1212, ext. 123, or visit www.yoursite.com"

This is pretty basic, but it gets all the points across in a very small ad. The title of the Bookmercial is the headline, then there's a very brief summary reiterating that it's "free," and then the phone number or website to place the order.

Here are some other typical lead generation headlines:

"How to Minimize Risk in Implementing Enterprise Resource Planning Systems"

"How to Protect Your Company from
Frivolous Lawsuits"

"How to Protect Your Global Information Systems
from Hackers, Adware, and Intrusion Threats"

"The Consumer Guide to Cosmetic Surgery"

"The CIO's Guide to Fiber Optic Networking"

These topics are targeted to the ideal prospect. As such, they are very narrowly focused. You don't need to draw everyone's attention to your offer, just the prospects that are in the education process about a subject you are an authority figure on.

Long Version Lead Generation Advertising

A long version ad isn't that much different. The best-known form of it is called an "advertorial." You see these a lot in magazines, where the copy looks like an article, but is a paid advertisement. It's very similar in format to a Bookmercial. It's half content and half advertisement.

As I said before, ads that don't look like ads tend to get noticed more. The long lead generation advertisement starts off like an article, using a catchy opening for the first paragraph, and then leads readers through the who, what, where, when, why, and how of the subject being written about. Toward the end, there is an offer for a free report or book on the topic along with the necessary contact information.

Again, this format works well when you're appealing to prospects that are in the information-gathering stage. They are more likely to read your advertorial, because the content is of interest to them and addresses the topic they are researching.

If you're advertising your Bookmercial in a trade publication or a magazine where the majority of readers are your prospects, offer it for free. Mention that shipping and handling is free as well. You don't want to put up even the smallest roadblock to a prospect getting your Bookmercial. Remember, the point of the book is to establish credibility, so a few dollars for shipping is a very inexpensive lead generation cost.

If you're advertising in a publication with mass appeal, charge for the shipping and handling as a filter. It will keep the freebie seekers from ordering your book simply because it's free.

Lead Generation "Advertising" in Multiple Media

The premise of the lead generation advertising approach is the idea that if you offer something useful and free as the first step in a business relationship, more people will say, "yes" to you and your company.

This approach can be used in a variety of media and delivery formats. For example, you can send a letter to your prospects offering them a free copy of your Bookmercial:

Dear Joe,

I noticed that you are a subscriber to *Industry Trade Monthly*. My name is John Doe and I'm the author of the book XYZ. I'd like to send you a free copy of my book where you'll discover:

- The basics of XYZ industry
- The 10 most common myths demystified
- The 5 key criteria to use when considering vendors in XYZ market
- The 3 biggest mistakes made by customers
- The best ways to get the most from a tight budget
- The 5 biggest rip-offs in XYZ industry that you must avoid

To request this free book, simply call 800-555-1212 x123 or visit www.mycompany.com/freebook123.

Sincerely,
John Doe

This same approach can be used when giving a speech. At the end of the speech, you can say the following:

"I hope you've enjoyed my talk today. As an attendee of XYZ event, they have arranged for all of you to receive a free copy of my book titled ABC. It's quite a useful reference that I recommend you all read. Inside the book, you'll discover:

- The basics of XYZ industry
- The 10 most common myths demystified
- The 5 key criteria to use when considering vendors in XYZ market
- The 3 biggest mistakes made by customers
- The best ways to get the most from a tight budget
- The 5 biggest rip-offs in XYZ industry that you must avoid

To request a free copy of this book, just drop your business card in the fishbowl in the back. Thanks, everyone, and have a great day."

You can also put the same message on your website. This is especially effective if your customer won't buy from a website without some offline interaction.

By offering to send your website visitors a free copy of your Bookmercial, you change the tone of the relationship from adversarial (salesperson vs. customer) to one that's more collaborative (teacher vs. student).

This approach also ensures that when your sales staff call to follow up, they will be received much more warmly than if they called in out of the blue.

Lead Generation Advertising Counters the Five Major Trends That Disrupt Traditional Marketing

The combination of a Bookmercial paired with lead generation advertising is more effective than image and one-step advertising. This is especially the case when you're trying to establish yourself with prospects as an authority figure. It also addresses some of the problems caused by the five mega trends that are making traditional marketing less effective.

In an age of advertising overload, lead generation advertising offers knowledge – not sales – within a traditional advertising space. To the prospect, your ad provides access to free and useful content (while still furthering your sales process behind the scenes), not just the typical sales language that you find in most advertisements and ignore.

In an age of distrust, lead generation advertising helps build trust first before trying to accomplish anything else. The prospect doesn't have to hand over a dime to you (except if you're charging the small shipping fee) to acquire a free sample of your knowledge and expertise. You don't have to say you're trustworthy. Prospects will discover this for themselves by seeing, feeling, and reading your Bookmercial. Once they trust you, they're much more likely to trust your company, too.

Prospects will find the fact that you're a published author reassuring. They will be disarmed by the fact that you're sincere in your efforts to help them achieve their objectives. In short, they will trust you a whole lot more than someone or some company that decides to skip trust building and move straight to a sales presentation. Finally, people listen, believe, and act upon the guidance of people they trust. Never underestimate this fact.

In an age of informed customers, customers seek to be informed so that they will not be ripped-off by a salesperson. The customer is the good guy. The salesperson is the bad guy. The traditional approach is adversarial. When you provide prospects with a Bookmercial through a lead generation advertisement, you become their partner in information gathering. You and your company are no longer the enemy. You are on the buyer's side. When you do a fantastic job of meeting the customer's information gathering needs, their confidence in your ability to meet their product and service needs goes up substantially.

In an age where the messenger is more influential than the message, your Bookmercial proves that you're a messenger worth paying attention to. When you've established yourself as a credible messenger, your message gets heard and acted upon. When you don't, your message gets ignored.

Finally, in the age of substance, lead generation advertising allows you to attract the largest possible audience for your Bookmercial. Without the space constraints of an expensive advertisement, you have the opportunity to tell your whole story and to explain the substance behind your products and services. This advantage must not be underestimated.

It's the equivalent of forcing your competitors to make their sales case in two minutes, while you get two hours. When prospects are reading about you and listening to you, they are ignoring your competitors at the same time. He (or she) who gets the most "air time" with a customer often wins. Lead generation advertising gets you the largest audience possible. Your Bookmercial gets you the "air time."

CHAPTER 11

How to Close More Sales More Quickly

By now, you're starting to see how a Bookmercial can generate leads, instill credibility, establish authority, and build trust. Now let's discuss the three ways it enables your sales team to convert a higher percentage of prospects to buyers and to shorten the sales cycle. This is perhaps the most important aspect to discuss, since the goal of nearly every business is to increase profitable revenues.

Method I: Improving Sales Conversion While Shortening the Sales Cycle

A Bookmercial enables your sales team to improve and shorten sales cycles. Let's look at each step of the customer's buying process to see how a Bookmercial gives your team a statistical edge at every level.

Here's a typical buyer's purchasing process:

1. Seek out information on product category
2. Gather information on the basics
3. Determine purchasing criteria
4. Seek out vendors and compare to purchasing criteria
5. Make purchase decision

Step 1: Seek Out Information on Product Category

The combination of lead generation advertising and a Bookmercial perfectly matches the needs of prospects in step 1 of their buying process. When you're able to offer the prospects exactly what they want, you get more of them engaged in an initial relationship with your company.

Step 2: Gather Information on the Basics

Your Bookmercial provides information on "the basics" of what a prospect needs to know about your industry in a single, well-organized source. When you do a thorough job of this, two things happen.

First, you dramatically reduce prospects' need to gather additional information from another competing source, keeping a higher percentage of prospects actively engaged with your company versus a competitor.

Second, since all the information they need is provided in your Bookmercial, it dramatically shortens the amount of time prospects need to spend gathering information on the basics.

Ultimately, this gets and keeps more prospects in your sales process and speeds up the prospects' ability to shift from "learning mode" to "buying mode."

Step 3: Determine Purchasing Criteria

While you provide your prospects information on the basics, you also subtly influence their purchasing criteria. Here's the main idea. You want to lay out all the important purchasing criteria prospects should be considering. Next, you point out their options and provide a real pros/cons assessment of each option. Finally, you go into a lot more detail on the option you want them to prefer (because it will ultimately favor your company) while still providing enough information to allow prospects to figure out if your solution is a good fit for them or not.

If you're a small company, you want to say something along these lines:

"Looking at the size of the vendor is an important consideration. The advantage of going with a big company is they tend to be well known, which some people find reassuring. However, going with a smaller company has numerous advantages. First, you'll have more clout with a smaller company. You'll be a major account and won't get lost in the shuffle. Second, smaller companies tend to focus more on customizing solutions to your specific needs. In comparison, big companies tend to force-fit 'one size fits all' solutions because this approach is easier for them to manage, even if it doesn't quite meet all of your needs."

Here's another example. Earlier in this Bookmercial, I mentioned that a Bookmercial is not a useful tool for companies selling low-price-point products – especially those purchased on an impulse basis. I mentioned this for several reasons.

First, the statement is true. Even though I have a vested interest in promoting Bookmercial books, deliberately attracting prospects that should rightfully be looking elsewhere is a waste of their time and mine. Second, even though I mention a point that doesn't favor my company or me, I don't dwell on it or go into much more detail. For example, I don't talk about what kinds of marketing tools would be appropriate for low-ticket impulse purchase type products. I simply state a Bookmercial is not for you, and quickly move on.

You'll also recall that I mentioned a Bookmercial is quite useful for companies selling high-ticket, complex products and services. This statement is also true. But unlike the earlier one, this statement favors my company. Because of this, I deliberately elaborated on it and explained the point in much more detail – in some cases, pages and pages of detail.

I go into detail because I want to ensure that my prospects put on their purchasing criteria list: "Choose marketing vehicle that's well suited for selling high-ticket, complex products and services." This happens to be what my company specializes in doing, and I also happen to know that the other advertising and marketing options available to my prospects are not optimized for this focused objective.

By talking about this point generically, I'm able to influence the prospects' purchasing criteria without having to mention anything specific about my company just yet. This behind-the-scenes look aside, generic "rules of thumb," like picking the right marketing vehicle that's specifically designed for your situation, come across as educational content (which it is) while still furthering the sale in my favor.

This approach fulfills the educational mission of identifying both sides of each option, but fulfills your sales mission by going into more detail on the option you would prefer them to want. With each criterion that you explain, you nudge their preferences closer and closer toward favoring your company.

This causes a higher percentage of prospects to seek product and service attributes that ultimately are in alignment with what your company can offer. It also enables prospects to figure out what they want much more quickly than if they were left on their own to sift through all the conflicting and confusing information in your marketplace.

Step 4: Seek Out Vendors and Compare to Purchasing Criteria

Next in the customer's process is to seek out vendors

to evaluate, comparing them to the purchasing criteria you helped shape. When you've done a good job of educating your prospects on the basics and helped them figure out what they want, often they will be less likely to consider other vendors. Since they trust you and know your company can fulfill all their needs, you become the default provider.

Faced with the option of either doing business with you and your company – a trusted and known entity – or having to deal with a bunch of additional vendors that may or may not be trustworthy, many will just take the easiest route and do business with your company.

Even those who do some comparison shopping will discover that nobody else seems to match their purchasing criteria and will favor doing business with your company.

In other words, the Bookmercial puts your company in the position of being the default provider and gets your company to that position more quickly.

Step 5: Make Purchase Decision

Finally, the prospect is ready to buy. While you and your sales team still need to close the sale, the prospect's overwhelming bias at this point is to buy from your company. It's worth pointing out that the prospect also has an overwhelming bias to ignore your competitors. In this kind of environment, all odds favor your company. It makes it a lot easier to close sales when the prospect has been properly educated and prepared to do business with you.

Method II:
Accelerating the Multi-Decision-Maker Sale

There's a specific type of sales situation that seems difficult for many salespeople. That's the multi-decision-maker sale. In the consumer world, this would be a purchase that involves getting a husband and wife to agree on a purchase. In the business-to-business world, it involves getting multiple executives to agree on a single purchasing decision. For example, a new marketing software system would need approval from the VP of Marketing, Chief Financial Officer (CFO), and Chief Information Officer (CIO).

There are two major problems caused by the multi-decision-maker sale. First, often your salespeople do not have direct access to all of the decision-makers. If your contact is the Chief Information Officer, he or she may not want you to bypass him or her in contacting others in the organization. Some prospects don't like outsiders messing around with the internal politics and will be alienated if someone tries to work around what they see as their role and job.

Second, much of the selling in multi-decision-maker sales occurs between the prospect and his or her peers. Continuing our earlier example, it may be the CIO that is presenting (a.k.a. selling) your product or service to the CFO and VP of Marketing. The problem with this is they usually aren't as good at promoting your products and services as you and your sales staff would be.

The reason these situations cause traditional salespeople problems is because their role must shift.

Instead of trying to close the deal themselves, they need to become sales coaches that coach their prospect on selling your company's products or services within the prospect's organization.

So to succeed in this environment, you don't want your salespeople to "sell harder" – you want them to "train their prospects how to sell" and provide the prospects with the sales tools to get the job done.

One of the best sales tools in this situation is a Bookmercial. Often, it's easier to get your Bookmercial passed around within the organization than to get your salesperson the access to do the same. Your Bookmercial represents your company's best effort at producing a "soft sell" of your company's products and services and is typically written for a "C-Level" executive audience, such as CEO, CIO, or CFO.

Since the Bookmercial looks and is educational in nature it tends to float to the top of the pile in terms of reference materials used for internal decision-making. Your Bookmercial speeds up the multi-decision-maker sale by being the salesperson inside your prospect's organization in situations where your live salesperson can't get in.

Method III:
Improving Sales Force Productivity

The simplest way to double sales in most organizations is to double the amount of time your salespeople are spending in front of highly qualified prospects. An outside salesperson may spend only 90 minutes a day actually in front of the right kind of prospect. The rest of the time is spent traveling, dealing with gatekeepers, or meeting with prospects that aren't qualified. If you take that outside salesperson, and get him or her in front of the right kind of prospect 180 minutes a day, often you stand a good chance of doubling sales.

The same is true with telephone-based salespeople. If they are on the phones six hours a day, but spend five hours dealing with gatekeepers, voicemail systems, and prospects that can't talk right now, they may spend only an hour a day actually speaking to a prospect. If you can double that time to two hours, the potential to double sales goes up significantly.

One way to double the productivity of your sales force is to shift the burden of dealing with early-stage prospects to your Bookmercial. Let your Bookmercial sift through your prospects for you and focus your sales staff only on those prospects most interested in your products and services.

For example, if your sales team spent the majority of their time with people who have already read your Bookmercial, their sales numbers will go up significantly. This happens for two reasons. First, a prospect that takes the time to read a Bookmercial is obviously very interested in solving his or her problem. Anytime your sales team spends a greater portion of their day with very serious prospects, as opposed to prospects that are "just looking," their numbers will go up. A more qualified prospect pool always increases sales.

Second, the Bookmercial does 50 to 70% of the sales job for you. In other words, Bookmercial readers are largely "pre-sold." This allows your sales team to be more effective in their sales efforts – essentially just closing sales opportunities that are already half-done. This is, of course, less work than selling a prospect from scratch. Any time you can cut the difficulty level of a sale in half, it cuts the time needed to close the sale in half. This allows the same size sales force to handle twice as many prospects and deals. This not only grows sales, but also improves profitability dramatically because you're driving top line sales without adding to your fixed overhead expenses.

Section IV: How to Produce a Bookmercial

CHAPTER 12

A Bookmercial Isn't Written, It's Engineered

In this section, we will discuss what's needed to produce a Bookmercial and what options are available to you. The simplest way to appreciate the process of creating a Bookmercial is to compare it to the process used to write a traditional book.

The goal of a traditional book is to inform – to convey knowledge from the author to the reader. The goal of a Bookmercial is purely and solely to increase revenues for your company. The two objectives are not the same. Therefore, the process used to meet each objective differs as well.

It's Not About the Book, It's About Solving Revenue Growth Problems

The process of producing a Bookmercial starts with a clear analysis of your company's market position, lead generation process, and sales systems. This is always the starting point for a Bookmercial – figuring out what part of your sales and marketing process you are trying to improve. Let me explain the reason why every Bookmercial project should begin with understanding the business problem that needs to be solved.

A book, or Bookmercial for that matter, is simply a tool. A tool is only useful when it is applied to a specific problem. For example, a hammer that sits in a toolbox has no value. However, a hammer that's actively used to build an addition to a house is useful.

There is an ideal tool that's well suited for every problem. A hammer is best used for connecting two pieces of wood together with nails. A saw is best used for cutting a piece of wood in half. Similarly, a Bookmercial can be optimized to solve one type of revenue growth related problem over another. Since a Bookmercial has this flexibility, you need to define the problem clearly up front.

Start with Clear Objectives

To start, forget temporarily about the Bookmercial topic, its title, and its content. While all of that will need to be addressed, the starting point is to give specific thought to what problem or problems you want to solve with your Bookmercial.

While a Bookmercial is a flexible tool, it does have its limitations. While it can solve any one of a dozen revenue growth related problems, it can't necessarily solve all of them simultaneously. Before anything is written, you want to clearly identify and prioritize which problems you want to solve with the Bookmercial.

This list of prioritized objectives is then used as the basis for every decision in the Bookmercial production process. The selection of titles, content, sequencing of content, specific choice of words, printers, distribution methods, scheduling options, staffing, and countless other decisions are all driven by your list of objectives.

Different objectives result in different outcomes. The importance of determining your ideal outcome determines how your entire Bookmercial should be produced.

Staff Your Bookmercial Team with the Skills to Meet the Objective

Once you have the objective in mind, you'll want to staff your team to best accomplish the objective. Here's the golden rule to staffing that will ensure a successful project. Don't staff a team to write a book; staff a team that's accustomed to solving the revenue growth problem you're trying to solve.

Here's an example.

Bookmercial books are often used in companies that sell goods and services to "C-Level" executives in other companies, such as the Chief Executive Officer (CEO), Chief Financial Officer (CFO), Chief Information Officer (CIO), or Chief Marketing Officer (CMO). In these situations, your team should consist of people who are familiar with communicating with people in those positions or have been in those positions previously.

The Executive Editor Role

You want someone on the team who has had extensive experience being in the shoes of the reader. In addition, it's important that this person have no prior experience with your company – just like your reader.

In my company, we call this role the Executive Editor. If the book's intended audience is a Chief Financial Officer, then the Executive Editor we typically use is a Harvard Business School graduate and former interim Chief Financial Officer of a $1 billion a year division of a Fortune 500 company.

If the book's intended audience is a Chief Information Officer, the Executive Editor we typically use is someone who has been in the role of Chief Information Officer of a business that's now a public company.

Since most of my company's work is for business-to-business companies, we have Executive Editors to cover the roles of CEO, CFO, CIO, and CMO. In situations where we don't have the right Executive Editor on staff, we will find the right person for the project.

If you're wondering why we go to so much trouble, and why you should too, the answer is simple. The purpose of a Bookmercial is to solve a specific revenue growth problem, usually by influencing a particular type of prospect to take the next step in your sales process. In these situations, it's nearly impossible to influence that target reader if you don't have first-hand knowledge of how they think, behave, and act.

Before your prospect ever reads a Bookmercial, you want to make sure that one of his or her peers has validated the fact that the Bookmercial will accomplish its intended objective.

The Revenue Growth Advisor

The role of the Revenue Growth Advisor focuses on analyzing the specific revenue growth problem in the company and custom tailors the Bookmercial to address those specific needs. For example, if a company is complaining that prospects are confusing the company's message with its competitors, the Revenue Growth Advisor might recognize this as a market-positioning problem. This type of problem occurs when a company's self-description uses a specific choice of words that happens to invoke an immediate (often undesirable), pre-conditioned psychological response from the prospect. To solve this problem, new marketing terminology needs to be invented and used to bypass this problem and solve the underlying revenue growth problem.

For example, in the early days of the automobile industry, the auto manufacturers' marketers referred to their products as "horseless carriages." While this is a technically accurate description, it caused confusion in the marketplace. The reason this happened is because readers already had a pre-defined notion of a carriage (it's the thing that goes behind a horse), so every time marketers used the term, the more confused prospects became.

The solution in the automobile industry's case was to invent the term "automobile." At the time, nobody knew what an automobile was, which was actually a good thing, because it gave the industry an opportunity to define it. In this case, it was easier to define a new term than trying to change the meaning of an old term.

On a Bookmercial team, it is the role of the Revenue Growth Advisor to notice any one of a dozen common revenue growth problems and adjust the Bookmercial creation plan or content to prevent or fix these problems.

Other common revenue growth problems the Revenue Growth Advisor identifies and solves are:

- Prospects don't perceive a difference between a company and its competitors.

- The company's advantage over its competitors is multi-faceted and doesn't come from just one source. While this benefits customers enormously, it is difficult to covey in an easy and simple way.

- Once prospects get to know a company, they tend to buy, but the company finds it difficult to get a prospect's attention.

- The company's sales force has an easy time getting initial meetings with prospects, but difficulty closing sales.

- The company's sales force closes sales once they get a meeting with a prospect, but has difficulty getting meetings.

- Prospects have bought into a competitor's "view of the world" as to what's important to look for in a solution, and in such a world view, the company isn't perceived favorably.

These are common problems companies face in their markets. A Revenue Growth Advisor should be familiar with all of these issues and how to solve them. There are very few business problems that have not been experienced by another company (often in another industry) and successfully resolved. The role of the Revenue Growth Advisor is to bring proven approaches to resolving any type of revenue growth problems you may be facing.

It's also important to recognize that oftentimes the solution to fixing these problems has nothing to do with a Bookmercial itself. A Bookmercial is a highly effective tool for getting attention and telling your company's story. If your company's story has a major flaw in it (the type a Revenue Growth Advisor would recognize and assist you in resolving), the Bookmercial will get attention and communicate the flaw to your marketplace. Obviously, this is not a good thing.

The role of the Revenue Growth Advisor is to worry about the big picture of how your Bookmercial fits in with everything else you're doing. Once again, it's not about the book, it's about solving the revenue growth problem.

The Sales Strategist

The next role you want on the team is someone we call the Sales Strategist. This role is someone who has a proven track record of developing the persuasion architecture of a Bookmercial. From the first word to the last word of a Bookmercial, each word is chosen deliberately as part of an overall "soft-sell" sales campaign.

This role requires someone who has a proven track record in sales (not sales copy or sales writing, but actual sales), has mastered the nuances of selling through words, knows the subtle differences that linguistics and word choice have on persuasive power, and is accustomed to influencing the intended reader (such as a C-level executive).

Developing the persuasion architecture is vitally important in achieving the commercial objectives of the Bookmercial. Developing a 150-page "soft-sell" Bookmercial takes a gentle, yet highly sophisticated touch. The Sales Strategist uses two key tools as part of this process.

Tool #1: Target Customer Belief System Analysis. The first is a belief system analysis of the target customer. The purpose of this analysis is to identify the prospect's current belief system. It's important to do so because this represents the starting point of the persuasion campaign. It's impossible to persuade a reader to your point of view if you do not know the reader's current point of view.

Here's a simplified example of a belief system analysis. The typical prospect might believe that:

1. Only big companies are reliable enough to do business with.

2. Extended service contracts are not important for this type of purchase.
3. For this type of product, lowest price is the most important thing.

Tool #2: Identifying the Desired Belief System You Want Customers to Have. In addition to analyzing the reader's current belief system, the Sales Strategist will work with team members to determine the belief system that prospects must adopt to achieve the stated objectives for the Bookmercial.

Let's assume that the client company may be one of the smaller providers in his or her market. Since the company is smaller and doesn't have the volume and efficiencies to compete in offering the lowest price product, it competes through the free services it provides with its products. Its products may be designed for easy remote diagnostics, maintenance, and repair. While the total price of its solution is more expensive than the competition, the client's solution is a better deal over a three-year ownership period.

In this situation, a prospect will only buy from the client if he or she believes that:

1. The best solution in this category of product is a customized solution, and only small companies in the market offer customized solutions (the big companies only offer generic solutions).

2. Unexpected repair and maintenance costs make the actual cost of ownership higher than the initial purchase price.

3. The lowest total cost of ownership (inclusive of repair and maintenance costs) over a three-year period should be the primary buying criteria (not the initial purchase price of the product itself).

Influencing the Prospect's Belief System. The next step in the process for the Sales Strategist is to identify a method for closing the gap between the prospect's current belief system and the belief system you'd like him or her to have. Creating a persuasion architecture that leads prospects from their current beliefs to the new set of beliefs is how this is accomplished. One of the secrets of doing this effectively is to take many "baby steps" in the persuasion process.

If the Bookmercial starts off with an arrogant tone that tells readers everything they believe to be true is dead wrong, it's too much of a leap too fast. The typical person cannot make such a dramatic shift in beliefs that quickly. The first reaction to this overwhelming approach is to resist it. The more effective approach is to spoon-feed prospects small bite-sized pieces of information that change their mind one step at a time. This is more effective than presenting new information all at once that completely contradicts the prospect's understanding of the situation. The incremental approach results in the prospect being more likely to adopt and act on the new beliefs.

For example, if part of the persuasion architecture requires convincing the prospect of the advantages of going with a small company, here's what an effective persuasion architecture will look like.

The architecture always starts by initially reinforcing the prospect's pre-existing beliefs. You don't tell prospects they are wrong as a used-car salesman would do; you tell them they are right. Then you might make a baby step argument (either an explicit argument or, more commonly, a simple story or parable that makes the same point) that the prospect's mostly right, but there are a few exceptions. Then you explain the exceptions.

If we need to take a prospect that believes he or she should work only with a big company, we might say, "It's a good idea to work with big companies. They have a major presence in their markets and are known entities. Their products are well established, and consistent in their design and capabilities from year-to-year. Whatever you buy this year, you can be assured you'll be able to buy the same product next year."

The argument might continue as follows: "However, there are a few circumstances where buying from a big company might not be the best choice. For example, if you need your system to be flexible enough to meet your specific needs, then products from big companies often aren't appropriate. Big companies focus on developing inexpensive "one-size-fits-all" products, leaving it to the smaller companies to serve clients with more specific needs."

The Details Matter. You'll notice that the preceding example uses words like "might not be the best choice" instead of "wrong" and "aren't appropriate" instead of "are a bad idea." There's a deliberate reason for this. If your sales and marketing message strongly contradicts the prospects' viewpoint, or if the message is worded too directly, prospects often take that as a personal criticism. Psychologically speaking, it makes them feel uncomfortable that they, their decisions, or their ideas are wrong. It's better to say that it's a reasonable point of view, but often people commonly forget to consider X, Y, or Z. So a prospect is never "wrong," they are "right, but…"

This may seem like an unusual level of detail for our discussion here, but I mention it for two important reasons. First, extensive psychological research shows that if decision-makers are challenged on their previous beliefs and decisions in an adversarial way, the "attack" actually reinforces their pre-existing belief. In short, if you tell someone they are not just wrong, but "dead wrong," "totally wrong," or they "couldn't be more wrong," they actually believe and stick to their previous beliefs even more.

Second, extensive research by the polling companies used by political candidates to win elections shows something interesting. They've found that by changing just a single word or phrase in a candidate's position creates dramatic statistical differences in their popularity. In other words, in the marketplace for ideas (whether political or commercial), the difference between success and failure often comes down to a single word. Words matter. You must ensure your team picks them extremely carefully.

Going back to our example, this sales strategy carefully nudges a prospect's belief system from where it is today to where the company needs it to be by the end of the Bookmercial. If you take the example above and multiply it 15 to 30 times, you start to get a feeling for what effective persuasion architectures are designed to do.

In addition, often there is a deliberate sequencing as to which beliefs to influence and in which order. Often, the reason a particular idea appears on page 15 of a Bookmercial is to introduce a concept that's needed to persuade the reader of a key idea on page 72.

This is what the Sales Strategist does – lays out all the pieces of a compelling sales argument that is not just logically clear but also emotionally and psychologically acceptable to the prospect. It takes all three to get the job done, and you want someone on your team who is accustomed to fulfilling this role, particularly as it applies to the written word.

Traditional Book Writing Team

In addition to the roles of Executive Editor, Revenue Growth Advisor, and Sales Strategist, you will need access to a book writing team. This team typically involves a writer or ghostwriter, several editors, and many proofreaders. In addition, your team will need a project manager and one or more graphic designers to lay out the Bookmercial body content and book cover.

Marketing and Publicity Team

Finally, you'll need a marketing and publicity team to get the most value out of your Bookmercial. For many of our clients, their in-house marketing team incorporates the new Bookmercial into their existing marketing efforts. Often, this in-house team is supplemented with training or consulting services from an expert in Bookmercial marketing.

Other times, the client will outsource some of their marketing and publicity efforts to a specialist in the field of using Bookmercial books to generate media inquiries or prospects.

As you can see, the process of producing a Bookmercial is an elaborate, deliberate, and thoughtful process. It starts by identifying the revenue growth obstacles that a Bookmercial needs to overcome. It requires an extensive team that specializes in solving revenue growth problems rather than just a traditional book writing team.

When you have clear goals, a proven process, and an experienced team working on your Bookmercial, you tend to get great results. If the goals are murky, the process you use isn't proven, or you have a team that's not experienced in solving the kind of revenue growth problems you have, the results tend not to be good.

CHAPTER 13

How to Choreograph Bookmercial Content

While a Bookmercial is engineered to solve a specific set of revenue growth problems, there's also an element of "art" within a process that's mostly a "science."

As I've mentioned earlier in this book, a Bookmercial consists of two types of content: 1) educational content that answers your prospects' frequently asked questions; and, 2) content that leads your prospect down a path that results in them doing business with your company.

The artistry of writing a Bookmercial comes from interweaving these two types of content into a single and cohesive book. Here's an easy way to understand how this appears to the reader. Imagine that every sentence that's purely educational is printed in white text, and everything that's sales oriented is printed in red. Done properly, the color of the text in the Bookmercial starts as pink until the last few pages where the text becomes a clear red.

In other words, from the very first word, the educational and sales content is artfully blended together to be largely indistinguishable from one another. Initially, there is no reference to your products or services at all. This makes the Bookmercial feel and read like any useful reference book.

Toward the middle of the Bookmercial, readers will start seeing a few case studies and examples used to illustrate specific concepts they need to understand. Of course, those case studies will mention (but not sell) your company's products or customers. This allows readers to begin absorbing relevant information about your company as part of an open-minded, educational experience, rather than as part of a close-minded, adversarial sales experience. Toward the end of the Bookmercial, the reader will start seeing a shift to more explicit sales content. The Bookmercial typically then ends by asking the prospect to take the next step in your sales process – typically a phone meeting, in-person meeting, or initial evaluation of some type.

The Dual Mission of a Bookmercial

The mission of the Bookmercial is to create an informed customer that is led to do business with your company. Both the educational and persuasive content are key components of a Bookmercial.

If you only create a traditional book, you simply create an educated customer that is excited to do business with your industry, but not necessarily your company.

If you only create a book with pure sales content (a brochure in disguise), your prospects will immediately be turned off and treat all the information in the disguised brochure as untrustworthy.

It's only through the artful choreography of weaving genuinely useful educational content together with deliberately considered persuasive content that you effectively increase revenues through your Bookmercial.

Educational Content Converts Prospects into Buyers

The educational information in the Bookmercial moves prospects from the "information gathering" phase to the "actively buying" phase of their buying process. You want to address those issues that are keeping them from deciding to buy. You want to walk them through each problem, explain options, dispel rumors, correct misinformation, and answer questions.

Questions are always one of the biggest sticking points in the minds of prospects. They have lots of them, and each one needs to be answered before you can get prospects to the next step. While you could answer them over and over again during a traditional sales cycle, you can answer them just once in a Bookmercial.

You also want to correct misconceptions and dispel rumors. These can be unnecessary roadblocks to any sale, since prospects often rely on their friends, associates, and the Internet for their research.

The same is true with anything that's confusing. This includes terminology, lingo, and jargon that many industries use to create mystery when they should be creating clarity instead.

You also want to address any fears you know your prospects have. If you know their fears, you can allay them by providing them with facts. An anxious prospect does not buy. Address their fears head-on and you'll put them at ease – helping them reach a buying decision more quickly.

The content needs to be presented in an order that is easy to follow and simple to understand. For instance, if you have several hundred frequently asked questions and simply create a long list, you'll overwhelm your prospects. Providing good information is not enough; it must be organized and structured in a way that can be absorbed easily.

The goal is to make the buying process surprisingly simple and easy for them. If the buying process seems too complicated, you risk causing them to procrastinate on the buying decision in favor of working on something else in their lives that's not so complicated.

By answering all the questions and putting the content together in a structure that makes sense, your Bookmercial sounds more like a how-to book than a sales piece. As a result, you end up sounding more like a teacher than a salesperson and, as we have noted elsewhere, teachers are more trusted than salespeople.

Persuasive Content Convinces Prospects Not to Buy from Just Anyone, But to Buy from Your Company

Persuasive content is the information you weave in throughout the educational content to steer clients to you. It has to be subtle, yet deliberate. Here's the reason.

The whole purpose of embedding your sales content within an educational book is to improve your chances of influencing readers.

People read educational information with an open mind and are more likely to consider information that contradicts their previous knowledge. These same people read overt sales information, like sales presentations and brochures, with a skeptical eye. In such an overt sales environment, any contradictory information is not accepted nearly as readily.

As you're putting your Bookmercial together, use the persuasion architecture mentioned earlier as your guide. Start working on influencing your prospect's general beliefs from page one, and then slowly move to influencing specific beliefs as the Bookmercial progresses.

Few people will make big shifts in their buying behavior in one massive step. Effective persuasion requires baby steps. You need to take them through these steps one at a time at a certain cadence. There is a rhythm to well-crafted persuasion so the prospect has a series of "a-ha" moments of discovery.

You'll notice that quite a bit of thought and work happens before the first word of a Bookmercial is ever written. Relatively speaking, it's easy to get words on paper. It's much harder to get the *right* words on paper that will solve your specific revenue growth problem.

CHAPTER 14

Writing a Bookmercial

Once the groundwork and content structure for a Bookmercial has been defined, now is the time to actually write it. Your three options are:

1. Do it yourself
2. Hire a ghostwriter to do this for you;
3. Hire a Bookmercial service that does everything for you (writing, editing, proofing, printing, and distribution).

Let's talk about each one individually so you can see the pros and cons of each option and which options are best for each kind of situation.

Option 1: Write the Bookmercial Yourself

Creating a Bookmercial can be a time-consuming process. For the first-time author, it can take anywhere from 300 to 600 hours to do all the groundwork (select a clear revenue-oriented objective, identify prospect belief systems, develop a sales strategy, turn your competitors strengths into weaknesses, and determine educational content that needs to be covered), write the content, edit the manuscript nearly a dozen times, format the content, and get it published.

For the do-it-all-yourself-oriented person that focuses on this full-time, it is a three to six month project. Keep in mind this total project time is still faster than for books that end up in bookstores, which typically take one to two years from concept to being on the shelf.

It's also worth keeping in mind that the most difficult work happens before the first word is written. You need to determine how you're going to move the reader's belief system from point A to point B through a deliberate series of small steps. Then you'll need to figure out how you're going to embed this sales strategy into an educational book. This involves developing and bringing to life the persuasion architecture I referenced earlier. You just can't tell people what they should believe. You need to lead them in small steps if you want them to accept it. You want to hold their hand while they figure out the path to making a decision themselves.

Writing the First Drafts

Once you have all this mapped out, you want to create your first draft. You can count on a total of typically seven to twelve drafts before you've finalized your Bookmercial. Every Bookmercial my company has worked on has always involved at least seven drafts before the project was finalized.

This is not creative writing. It is deliberate writing, engineered to bring a prospect closer to a sale. The Bookmercial typically contains 125 to 225 pages. It needs to be reviewed carefully, not only for spelling and grammatical errors, but also for clarity. Not a single word should be wasted.

During every revision cycle, you want to focus on different elements. For example, your first draft is meant to just get your main ideas down. Each subsequent draft focuses on a different element of the Bookmercial creation process. Common themes of editing rounds include: 1) educational completeness; 2) marketplace position of the company; 3) looking for and solving gaps or problems in sales logic; 4) analyzing the emotional and psychological state of the reader as each chapter progresses, making sure none of the leaps are too big or appear too quickly; and, 5) evaluating the sales strategy to move a buyer convinced he or she needs to buy from one of the vendors in your industry to one that insists on buying from your company.

This is, of course, in addition to typical editing activities, such as editing for grammar, spelling, concision, and clarity.

Title Selection

Picking a title is a much more sophisticated process than most people realize. While a book certainly is judged by its title, the title selection must fit within the context of the revenue growth problem you're looking to solve.

For example, if your goal is to grab the attention of a specific type of prospect, the more tailored and specific your title is to that audience, the better.

If your goal is to raise the profile of you and your company through publicity and expert quotes in articles, then a Bookmercial with a broader title is often more appropriate. The broader title qualifies you to provide expert commentary in a wider range of articles.

If your goal is to challenge conventional norms in your industry, then a controversial title that sparks debate (and garners you media attention, and keynote and panel speaking opportunities) is a better approach.

The key to title selection is to link the choice of titles back to the original objectives of your Bookmercial project. Great results often come from a sharp focus on clear objectives. Title selection is no exception to this rule.

Option 2: Hire a Ghostwriter

It you don't have the time or energy to write your own book, you may want to engage the services of a ghostwriter. There are many good ghostwriters in the marketplace today, and I've had the good fortune to work with many of them. When you have a straightforward writing assignment, ghostwriters are a useful resource worth using.

However, when it comes to a Bookmercial project that involves complex sales issues, solving revenue growth problems, and understanding sophisticated "C-level" executive audiences, ghostwriters aren't always a great resource.

The main limitation of ghostwriters is the fact that they are writers – not salespeople, former "C-level" executives, or marketing experts. Occasionally, you'll find a writer that describes him or herself as a copywriter. Often, these copywriters may have worked on writing a brochure but, fundamentally, don't know how to sell – especially complex products and services to "C-level" executive audiences. They haven't carried a revenue quota. They haven't closed multiple seven-figure deals. They haven't carried profit and loss responsibility for a sizeable company or division of a company.

Ghostwriters are accustomed to writing. They are not accustomed to solving revenue growth problems in complex sales and marketing organizations using tools that happen to involve writing. It's an important distinction to keep in mind. That's why you find a lot of writers that are not doing well financially. They write well, but they don't know how to sell, including selling their own services. Each type of writing – educational and persuasion – requires a different style, and finding a single person capable of doing both simultaneously can be difficult.

Tradeoffs aside, adding a ghostwriter to your team does reduce your workload. Instead of requiring you to commit 200 to 600 hours to your Bookmercial project, it'll probably be more like a 100 to 300 hour time commitment on your part.

If you use a ghostwriter, you should realize that you still must do about 35% of the work yourself, and it's the most important portion of the project. If you lay a poor foundation for your Bookmercial, it will not work.

A ghostwriter assists you in creating a Bookmercial, but it is not realistic to expect the ghostwriter to drive the process – especially linking the Bookmercial to solving a particular set of revenue growth problems.

There are still many things you need to be responsible for. This includes defining objectives, belief analysis, belief system objectives, troubleshooting revenue growth problems, developing the persuasion architecture, blending educational content with persuasive content, title selection, interior graphic design, book cover design, ISBN registration, book printing, book distribution, editing, proofreading, project management, and publicity.

As a point of comparison, when my company produces a Bookmercial on behalf of a client, the writer's role is just one of ten roles on the team. It certainly is an important one, but it's important to realize the role the writer plays is just one of many required roles.

Finally, you'll want to budget for the cost of a ghostwriter. A *New York Times* bestselling ghostwriter typically charges $200,000 for a book. You probably don't need someone with that caliber of skill. A full-time professional book ghostwriter will typically cost from $30,000 to $50,000 per book. They'll want six months to complete the project.

This excludes the cost of third-party editors and proofreaders (always a good idea, since it's very hard for a writer to spot his or her own typos), interior graphic design fees, book cover graphic design fees, and photography or image licensing fees. You'll want to budget up to another $15,000 for this, not to mention the cost of printing, setting up distribution, and fulfillment.

As you can see, this adds up to quite a project. Even with a ghostwriter and designer in the mix, you're still looking at 200 hours of your time, plus $45,000 to $65,000 in fees.

Option 3: Use a Bookmercial Production Company

Throughout this book, I've been referencing my own company's experiences in producing Bookmercial books. This is because we've been helping our clients solve revenue generation problems for some time now. In fact, we're the only company that produces a Bookmercial. Here's a little history on the birth of the Bookmercial and the process I've developed to produce them on behalf of clients.

The History of the Bookmercial

I originally developed the Bookmercial book format out of the frustration I felt as a marketer and buyer of complex technology products. As a customer, I found that dealing with salespeople and their marketing colleagues was often a waste of time. While a few added value to the sales and marketing process, most were simply out to get my money. I found it hard to trust anyone. I couldn't tell who was a genuine expert in the industry and who was not, and wasted too much time trying to sift through each company's claim that they're the best in the industry.

All I wanted was someone to provide me with genuinely useful information, help me understand all my options, and enable me (not them) to make a well-informed decision. I didn't think that was too much to ask, but apparently I was wrong.

As a marketing executive of technology products, I hated having my company lumped in with the noise. It didn't really matter if my company had something useful and exciting to offer if I couldn't get anyone to pay attention to it. In addition, prospects have become so distrustful of sales and marketing people that, whatever you say, their first instinct is to assume you're exaggerating. It was quite a frustrating experience.

I developed the Bookmercial format as a way to be different, to establish myself as an authority figure, and to promote whatever product or service I wanted to promote. I genuinely feel that the Bookmercial is a win-win solution for the customer and the marketer. The customer gets genuinely useful information that makes it much easier to make a well-informed decision quickly. For the marketer, a Bookmercial stands out as something obviously different from your run-of-the-mill, often ignored brochure. It also positions you as a true industry expert with the prospect (and the media, too) and warms up a business relationship quickly. It also gives you the room to tell your entire story and make it easy for prospects to seek you and your company out, rather than having your sales force hunt and chase them down.

In my experience, customers like the process of buying, particularly when you make it easy and low risk to do so. In contrast, they don't like the process of being sold, hunted, or chased by sales people. The Bookmercial gives people on both sides of the table precisely what they want.

The Bookmercial Production Service

Our Bookmercial production service enables clients to invest just 15 hours to have a Bookmercial produced on their behalf. This saves time in comparison to the 200 to 600 hours you'd invest writing a Bookmercial yourself, or even producing one with a traditional ghostwriter.

With less than two days of cumulative work, you can become a published author and use a high-quality Bookmercial to tackle your biggest revenue growth challenges. This small time investment is typically broken into chunks of three to four hours and entails doing a series of interviews with you, or you and your staff.

The first session focuses on understanding your current sales and marketing efforts. We'll want to know what's working well, what's not, and what you'd like to improve with a Bookmercial. We'll be asking you about your company's level of brand recognition in the marketplace, your competitors, how you generate leads, how easy or difficult it is to convert leads into buyers, in addition to dozens of other specific questions. Typical questions include:

- Who are you customers? What segments do you target? What makes your offering appealing to your target segments versus other market segments?

- What's the level of awareness your prospects have of your industry? Of your company specifically? Should the Bookmercial promote the industry in which you already dominate? Or is the industry already well known so the Bookmercial should focus instead on why someone should choose your company over your competitors?

- What type of customers do your competitors focus on? Are you trying to steal your competitors' prospects or simply trying to split the market (your company targeting one segment of customers, your competitors another)?

- Are you looking to promote your company overall, a particular product line, or a specific product?

- Are your best prospects novices to your industry or veterans?

- What are the biggest objections your prospects have in doing business with your company? How have you typically handled them? What has your success rate been?

- Who are you primary competitors? Is there an industry giant you compete against? If so, what are your advantages and disadvantages versus them? Are the differences major ones or minor ones?

- Are your primary sales bottlenecked early in the sale process or late? Is it easy for your company to make contact with prospects, but hard to close them? Or vice versa?

- What action do you want prospects to take after they receive your Bookmercial? Buy on the spot? Schedule a meeting or phone call with a salesperson? Visit a website?

This extensive examination of your sales and marketing process allows us to clearly define the problem you want solved with the Bookmercial. Once again, it's important to note that a Bookmercial can be custom tailored to solve a wide range of revenue growth problems, but only if those problems are known, defined, and part of the stated objectives of the project.

The next few interview sessions will focus on knowledge transfer from you and your team to ours. We'll want to gather all the frequently asked questions your prospects typically ask and their answers. We'll get a "brain dump" of the major products or services you want to promote.

The remaining time will be taken up with approvals, design issues, and reviewing the actual content of the book itself. With only two days worth of involvement on your part, you can have a Bookmercial written, printed, and in your hands within 60 days.

Producing a Bookmercial in Only 60 Days

One of the values we offer our clients is speed. You work in a competitive environment where speed matters. Most of our clients think waiting one to two years for a traditionally published book is way too long. Even the typical six-month turnaround time for a ghostwritten manuscript (that's not yet laid out, published, or printed) is too slow for most companies.

We're able to turnaround a Bookmercial project so quickly because we've developed a system expressly for this purpose. Our typical Bookmercial project is completed from start to finish in 60 days.

First, we take a team approach to Bookmercial production. In total, roughly 10 people will be involved in your Bookmercial project. These roles include the Executive Editor, Revenue Growth Advisor, Sales Strategist, Writer, Editors, Proofreaders, Interior Book Designer, Cover Designer, Project Manager, Client Service Manager, and Printing & Distribution Coordinator.

Second, we borrow principles from "just-in-time-manufacturing." For example, once the lead writer completes a chapter, the draft is turned over to others to edit, revise, proofread, edit, re-edit, and approve that chapter, even as the next one is being written. By the time the lead writer has finished the first draft of Chapter 4, a team of editors and proofreaders have created the final version of Chapter 3. With three to seven people working on a book simultaneously, the entire book is completed within days of finishing the first draft of the book.

In contrast, the traditional method of book writing looks more like a relay race—where only one member of the team is busy at any given time. The author finishes the first draft. He or she then hands off the manuscript to an editor. While the editor is working, the author is waiting. This time consuming process repeats itself many times with editors, proofreaders, and designers.

This approach is adequate for the slow-moving publishing industry, but generally unacceptable to CEOs and marketing executives of the companies we work with.

In our process, we still do the same steps, but rather than waiting for each person to finish the entire manuscript, we pass each chapter on down through the system as it's completed. One lead writer works on the overall Bookmercial to ensure a consistent voice, but the various rounds of editing and proofreading are all done concurrently to enable a much faster completion time without skipping any steps. The end result of this scheduling innovation is a much faster turnaround time than anything the traditional publishing industry is used to seeing.

It's an ideal option for someone who values solving revenue growth problems with a Bookmercial, but doesn't have the time to write and manage a Bookmercial project on his or her own.

CHAPTER 15

Printing and Distributing Your Bookmercial

Once your Bookmercial has been written, you need to get the Bookmercial printed and distributed to your target audience. There are four options:

1. Use a traditional book publisher for printing and distribution
2. Use a book printer for printing and self-distribute
3. Use a self-publishing company
4. Use a Bookmercial service for initial printing and distribution to online bookstores

Option 1: Use a Traditional Book Publisher

Before we go into other options, let's look at traditional book publishers. Traditional publishers, like Random House and McGraw-Hill, make their money exclusively from selling low-price-point books. This is inherently a low profit, high volume type of business.

The typical book publishing process with the larger houses takes 12 to 24 months. Books are produced at specific times during the year to coincide with major industry sales seasons. Three times a year, sales reps from the publishing houses go out to the various wholesalers and bookstores to get them to place orders for books scheduled to come out during that season.

On the positive side, getting a book published through a traditional book publisher is prestigious. In addition, if your book has mass-market appeal and you have a major marketing effort behind your book, a traditional publishing house can distribute a bestseller well.

However, working with traditional publishers has several downsides. First, if your topic is highly specialized, traditional publishers aren't interested, because they know you won't be able to sell enough books to make it worth their while. Second, traditional publishers don't like seeing commercial content inside their books. They see books as a stand-alone product rather than as a way to attract leads or pre-sell prospects for more expensive products and services. Third, the revenue performance standards that you as an author need to achieve to keep your book in stores is generally too high for a book on a specialized topic.

To understand the last point, you need to understand how the traditional book industry works. Traditional publishers do not market your book until after it's a bestseller. As the author, it's your job to drive book sales, and it's their job to make sure the book is on the shelf when you do. From the day of the book's initial release, you have 90 days to drive sales to an acceptable level. If you can't, the books are automatically returned to the publisher and sold in remainder houses for out-of-print books for pennies on the dollar.

This means you can invest 12 to 24 months to get a book through the process of a traditional publisher, only to have the book be on the shelves for 90 days. Considering it's often a major battle just to get your company's contact information into the book, going through traditional publishers does not have a good return on investment in terms of time or dollars. It's not an attractive option for anyone publishing a Bookmercial on a specialized topic.

Option 2:
Use a Book Printer for Printing and Distribute Your Book Yourself

The second model for printing and distributing your book is to use a book printer and distribute the book yourself. A printing company prints your book and sends the copies back to you to do with them what you please. In most cases, you can get your book back in several weeks or maybe a month.

The books are printed fairly inexpensively – $3 to $6 a copy, depending on quantity and turnaround time. This makes the book only slightly more expensive than a brochure, and certainly wins hands down on the impact it delivers per dollar spent.

The primary problem with using a printer is the printer only prints. You send them a file and they print it. They don't get involved in the creation of the book's content or ensuring your project is designed to solve specific revenue growth problems.

If you intend to use your book as a replacement for a brochure, then using a book printer is a good option.

If your objectives are broader than that, then using a book printer alone has some limitations. If you want to get them into online or brick and mortar bookstores as part of your marketing strategy, then using a book printer alone is not a very good choice.

Option 3: Use a Self-Publishing Company

The third method is to self-publish. There are some advantages and disadvantages to doing this. The greatest advantage of using a vanity publisher is they will assist you in distributing your books with the online bookstores. The project turnaround time is typically one to two months from the time you submit a completed manuscript and cover design for printing. If your book takes four months to complete, a vanity publisher will have it completed within six months.

In addition, vanity publishers do not provide the design work or writing, let alone any of the extensive work to ensure that your book solves the revenue growth problems you intend it to solve.

The benefit of using a vanity publisher is gaining access to online bookstores. The downside is if you intend to use the book as a replacement for a brochure, the cost is extraordinarily high. If your book retails at $20, it may cost you anywhere between $10 and $12 to buy a copy for your own use from the self-publishing company. In contrast, a stand-alone book printer will print the same book (but not distribute it) for only $3 to $6.

A vanity publishing company is ideal if your only objective is to ensure your book is for sale online and you have no other planned uses for the book (such as for lead generation or a brochure replacement).

Option 4: Use a Bookmercial Publishing Service

The final method is to use a Bookmercial publishing service. In my company, all of our clients' Bookmercial production projects include publishing services. This offers you the most amount of flexibility and the best of all worlds.

First, we manage the entire printing and distribution process on your behalf. Second, we don't hold your book "hostage," forcing you to pay high printing fees for life.

Here's how this process works in most cases. The majority of our clients would like to have their books made available for sale at the major online bookstores and to have them handy as a sales piece for their company.

Here's what we do to enable our clients to have low-cost printing options in both scenarios. First, we set you up with the major online bookstores so your book is available for sale online. There are multiple ways to handle this objective, depending on your needs. The turnaround time for online bookstore distribution ranges from 0 to 45 additional days, following the completion of the Bookmercial project. The timing depends mostly on what other requirements you may have that impact the approach used to secure online bookstore distribution on your behalf.

Second, we also set up your Bookmercial to be printed by a low-cost book printer. This makes the price per book low enough to be used in multiple aspects of your sales and marketing process. After printing a starter batch of books for you, we provide all the files used to you so you can handle reprints directly from the printer. This allows you to become self-sufficient. You can deal directly with the printer after the first run, so you can control quantities and pricing without having to be dependent on us. It just becomes a simple reprint job for the printer.

The goal of our Bookmercial publishing service is to make the process as trouble free as possible. This publishing service is included with all of our Bookmercial production projects and is customized to meet the needs of the individual client.

The nicest benefit of this service is we take care of everything for you, provide you with a "best of all worlds" option, and then turn everything over to you, so you're always in control of your Bookmercial and never beholden to anyone.

CHAPTER 16

How to Get Started

At this stage, you should have a pretty good understanding of your options for creating a book, and a Bookmercial, in particular. You should have a clear sense of what a Bookmercial can do for you to help solve revenue growth issues in your company.

A Bookmercial helps you to:

- Cut through the marketplace noise

- Demonstrate that you (and your company) are trustworthy

- Engage prospects in information-gathering mode with useful educational materials that pre-empt them from going to your competitors

- Make you the obvious expert in your field and identify you as someone worth paying attention to

- Create the room necessary to tell your entire story, showing what your company has to offer and how it's different from the competition

My company's Bookmercial production service was created with the mission to solve revenue growth problems through book publishing. Our services ensure you'll receive the right Bookmercial designed to solve your toughest revenue growth problems. In addition, we'll do everything on your behalf, get everything done right, and minimize the time that you need to be involved with the project. This allows you to focus on managing your company without distraction.

If you're interested in learning more about my company's 15-hour Bookmercial creation service, simply look in the resources section of the next chapter for our contact information.

The next step in the process is to schedule a brief phone consultation with us where you'll be able to learn more about our service. In turn, we'll be able to learn more about your business situation.

We only take on clients whose opportunities or challenges we feel comfortable addressing with a Bookmercial book. Since this differs for every client situation, we respectfully ask to learn more about your situation before making any commitments as to how we might be able to help.

To contact us, simply refer to the resources section of the next chapter for our contact information.

Section V: Resources

CHAPTER 17

Author Contact Information

To take the next step to see if commissioning a Bookmercial book is right for your company, simply contact us for a free initial consultation.

We'll evaluate your area of expertise and the revenue growth challenges you'd like to address with your Bookmercial to see if we're able to meet your objectives.

To request a free consultation, simply email my office at **victor@bookmercial.com** or call **650-472-2916 x115**.